Connecting Children with Children, Past and Present

Connecting Children with Children, Past and Present

Motivating Students for Inquiry and Action

Eula T. Fresch

Foreword by Keith C. Barton

HEINEMANN
Portsmouth, NH

Heinemann
A division of Reed Elsevier Inc.
361 Hanover Street
Portsmouth, NH 03801–3912
www.heinemann.com

Offices and agents throughout the world

The author and publisher wish to thank those who have generously given permission to reprint borrowed material:

Figure 2–1(a-d) is reproduced by permission of The Huntington Library, San Marino, California.

Figure 2–2 courtesy of the Denver Public Library, Western History Collection, Call Number X-11929.

Figure 2–3 courtesy of the Denver Public Library, Western History Collection, Call Number X-13959.

Figures 2–4 and 2–5 courtesy of the Montana Historical Society, Helena, call numbers 950880 and 981030.

Figure 2–6 courtesy of Sally J. Mello.

Figure 2–7 courtesy of National Anthropological Archives, Smithsonian Institution/Negative No. 55516.

Figure 2–8 courtesy of National Anthropological Archives, Smithsonian Institution/Negative No. 55517.

Figure 3–1 courtesy of Minnesota Historical Society.

Figure 3–3 courtesy of the Atlanta History Center.

credits continued on page 172

Library of Congress Cataloging-in-Publication Data
Fresch, Eula T.
   Connecting children with children, past and present : motivating students for inquiry and action / Eula T. Fresch.
        p.   cm.
Includes bibliographical references
    ISBN 0-325-00591-5 (alk. paper)
   1. Social sciences—Study and teaching (Elementary) 2. Children—Study and teaching (Elementary) I. Title.
    LB1584.F68 2004
    372.83—dc22

                                                        2003022624

Editor: Danny Miller
Production editor: Sonja S. Chapman
Cover design: Jenny Jensen Greenleaf
Author photograph: Kim Fuller, Salve Regina University
Compositor: Argosy
Manufacturing: Steve Bernier

Printed in the United States of America on acid-free paper
08 07 06 05 04   VP   1 2 3 4 5

*To my husband, Glenn, my son, David,
and my social studies methods students
at Salve Regina University*

Contents

Foreword

Educators continually face the challenging of moving from theory to practice. No matter how much we know about principles of learning, the nature of historical inquiry, and the need to prepare students for active citizenship, we still have to translate these into practical classroom activities. In fact, the more we know about teaching, the harder it may seem to put our ideas into practice: How can we engage students in inquiry, build on their prior knowledge, expose them to multiple perspectives, and meet state and national standards, all at the same time? This is a daunting task, yet many teachers accomplish it, often with energy, enthusiasm, and creativity. With a little guidance, many more teachers might be able to do so.

Eula Fresch's *Connecting Children with Children, Past and Present: Motivating Students for Inquiry and Action* helps provide this guidance. This work is based on key elements of current theory and research in social studies and history education, but rather than simply telling readers about these principles, Fresch illustrates how they can be applied in effective and motivating ways. Teachers will come away from this book with a wealth of resources for the classroom, as well as numerous practical strategies for helping students connect with historical materials. They should also come away with one more thing, perhaps the most important of all: A vision of what history education could be, one that will motivate them to seek out new resources and develop engaging activities throughout their careers.

One of the book's most distinctive features is its focus on the historical experiences of children. As Fresch points out, elementary and middle school students are interested in other children, and this can motivate them to learn about historical topics that might not otherwise be so captivating. But just as important, emphasizing children in history is a way of building on students' prior knowledge. Teachers often wonder how they can activate mental schemas on topics that students don't know much about yet. Sometimes it seems like there's nothing to build on, and many teachers have begun KWL charts only to find that students can't come up with anything to put in the "Know" category! The prior knowledge of children and young adolescents, however, usually revolves not around specific people or events in history, but around day-to-day experiences—how people live and how their lives are influenced by their social context. By focusing on the experience of children in the past, teachers stand a better chance of making connections to their students' own lives. They can then extend that knowledge by helping students see how children's experiences have differed in other times and places.

Another important feature of this book is its organization into units. It's tempting to teach history in sequential order, moving from one event to the next in lockstep fashion, particularly when most textbooks are organized this way—despite the fact that there is not a shred of evidence that this is necessary for students to make sense of the past. On the other hand, with the increasing importance of state standards, many teachers feel compelled to teach individual objectives as though they were a checklist, with no relationships among lessons. Neither of these approaches helps students understand the connections that are at the heart of history and social studies. The chapters in this book, though, tie together a variety of topics on the basis of important thematic elements, such as experiences of war, movement, labor, and rights. This can help students see connections between topics they might otherwise consider separate and unrelated, such as slavery and child labor. It also enables teachers to address the historical experiences of a wider variety of people. Organizing a unit around "movement" rather than "the Westward movement of pioneers" makes it possible to highlight topics like the seasonal migration of Native Americans, as well as their forced relocation. This kind of thematic organization also makes connections with the present more obvious, because people today still struggle with war, migration, forced labor, and the quest for human rights.

This focus on the present is one of the most exciting features of the book. If the study of history does not help us understand the world of today, then it is just trivia, and there is no reason to study it. Moreover, if the subject does not contribute to citizenship, then it fails to live up to the goals of social education. Most history educators claim that the subject fulfills these roles, but rarely do they explain how. They often seem to believe that if students simply know more about the past, they will magically become better people. This book, however, draws out these links clearly and directly, and it provides suggestions on how students can become more active citizens. When children learn about injustices in history, they often feel frustrated by their inability to go back in time and make things better. Eula Fresch shows how they *can* make things better, not in the past but today, and for that reason alone this book should be a treasured part of every teacher's library.

Keith C. Barton, Professor
Division of Teacher Education
University of Cincinnati

Acknowledgments

This book evolved with the help of many people and in a climate that encourages scholarship and creativity. For all of these I am extremely grateful. My book began with the encouragement of my colleagues in the education department at Salve Regina University. I am especially appreciative of Camille Allen, who is a model of scholarship and continually urged me to write about my research and teaching, and to Beverley Murphy, who encouraged me to involve my social studies methods students in the process. A very special thank you to Dr. Matthew Downey, who gave me the idea for my book.

My book continued to evolve with the participation and eagerness of my social studies methods students who introduced the children they were teaching to young people in history. Many thanks to them and to the cooperating teachers in the Newport schools who invited us into their classrooms.

The research for my book progressed more smoothly because of the expertise of the reference librarians at Salve Regina University's library and the children's reference librarians at the Newport Public Library. I am indebted to them and to friends and colleagues who were always on the lookout for information on children in history and children making contributions today.

The research and permission-to-use fees for photographs was partially funded with a grant from Salve Regina University. I am very thankful for this grant and for the technical support of Kenneth DeRouin in Design Services at Salve Regina University in relation to all of my book's photographs.

Many, many thanks to Heinemann and my editor, Danny Miller, whose enthusiasm, insights, and expertise guided my book to its completion. I also thank my production editor, Sonja Chapman, my copy editor, Jan Stanley, and Jenny Jensen Greenleaf, who designed the cover.

I am deeply grateful to my husband, Glenn, for his technical help and continual support, and to our son, David, for his encouragement.

Finally, I am indebted to all the young people who kept diaries, wrote letters, and made contributions to history or to our world today. I thank them for making this book possible, for they are the ones who inspired me to write it.

1
Children "Meeting" Other Children: A Natural Motivator

When I read to them from In the Path of War: Children of the American Revolution Tell Their Stories *(Adler 1998), they were shocked to hear what those children went through.*

This describes the reaction of students in a fifth-grade class as they listened to the experiences of children near their age who grew up during the Revolutionary War. A preservice teacher in my social studies methods course shared this when she was describing how she had dressed as a colonial woman and had the children sit around a pretend campfire eating johnnycakes while she read from this collection of primary sources. The students were eager to find out more about real, not fictional, children who lived in the past, and about the events that went on around them. As this young future teacher showed her excitement at discovering how motivated her students were to begin inquiring into the Revolutionary War period, I recalled the many times I had seen this same eagerness, whether the students were studying immigration, the civil rights movement, the pioneers, or some other topic or theme.

And why shouldn't our students be motivated by finding out about other real children? As teachers, we know that children are naturally curious about other children and their lives and experiences. I certainly was aware of this, as both a teacher and a parent. But it has only been during the past eight years that I have researched and actually used primary sources by or about real children, both historical and modern. It all started when I was looking through some of my back issues of *Social Education* and came across one that had a special section on children in history. After reading about some of the resources that are available and the successes that teachers have had in using these primary sources with their students, I couldn't wait to begin my own research and primary sources collection. As I collected resources, I shared them with my social studies methods classes, demonstrated ways of using them in the classroom, and encouraged my education students to use them in their field experiences and student teaching.

Using primary sources by or about children has been a major emphasis in my writing (Fresch 2001, 2002) and teaching because perhaps "children and youth are the last major group in United States society that remains largely deprived of historical identity and cut off from its historical roots as a group. Helping young students to understand that children also have a history stimulates their interest in the past and aids historical learning" (Downey 1986, 261). It also lets them know that they are an important part of history, too.

There is a wealth of fiction, including historical fiction, about children. Teachers use these works in literature-based social studies programs. But the real people our students study in social studies programs are adults. The little information about specific young people that may be included usually comes from secondary sources; only rarely does it come from primary sources created by or about children. Students read about Rosa Parks, but not about Claudette Colvin, a fifteen-year-old who was arrested for refusing to give up her seat on a bus nine months before Rosa Parks was arrested. They read about General Ulysses S. Grant, but not about nine-year-old Johnny Clem, who joined a regiment of the Union army as a drummer and by age eleven had become a lance corporal. Our students need to read and hear the stories and perspectives of all groups including adults and children, and to use both secondary and primary sources if they are going to construct a more complete picture of a time period or event. By approaching social studies this way, teachers enable students to meet many of the National Council for the Social Studies (NCSS) standards (1994). Three of the performance expectations for the theme "Time, Continuity, and Change" relate to the importance of students studying different perspectives. "The learner can: demonstrate an understanding that different people may describe the same event or situation in diverse ways . . . ; compare and contrast different stories or accounts about past events, people, places or situations . . . ; and demonstrate an understanding that people in different times and places view the world differently" (51).

In the introduction to his book *We Were There Too! Young People in U.S. History* (2001), Phillip Hoose relates a statement that one girl made to him about her United States history class: "We're not taught about younger people who have made a difference. Studying history almost makes you feel like you're not a real person" (vi). This comment made Hoose think about his own education. When he couldn't remember having read about anyone his age in history classes, he looked through textbooks and found that the girl was right. The books featured a few young people, like Pocahontas and Sacagawea, "But for the most part, to become historically real, to be remembered in a U.S. history book, you had to be an adult" (vi).

Matthew Downey, the guest editor of *Social Education*'s special section on children in history, writes about being invited to give a presentation on local history to a fifth-grade class. He showed slides on the history of the area and answered questions. In the time left, he read accounts that early settlers had written of their childhoods on the Colorado frontier. One was the memoir of a woman who had been the victim of a stagecoach robbery when she was a young girl growing up during the gold-mining era. The following week, Downey received thank-you letters that showed how intensely interested these fifth-graders were in the accounts.

> I liked you as a speaker the best. I liked you telling us about pioneer children because all the other speakers didn't tell anything about them.
>
> You were the first one to talk about kids. Thank you.
>
> I'm glad you talked about kids and not adults. I liked the story about the girl who got robbed on a stagecoach. (Downey 1986, 263)

From the many similar letters that he received, Downey concluded that it hadn't occurred to these students that children had helped settle the West. They were delighted to find out that people near their age had played a role in their state's history.

Using Primary Sources By and About Children

The most authentic way to help historical young people become "real" to our students is to use primary sources whenever possible. According to Cynthia Stokes Brown, a primary source is "any material created at the time of an event, or later from the memory, by someone in the event" (1994, 17). Photographs, diaries, and letters written by children, and adults' memoirs of their childhoods give our students the opportunity to be "historians" because they can construct their own interpretations of what they view and read. This active construction is emphasized in the NCSS standards. For example, one of the performance expectations for the theme "Time, Continuity, and Change" is that the learner be able to "identify and use various sources for reconstructing the past, such as documents, letters, diaries, . . . photos, and others" (NCSS 1994, 51). In her book *Seeking History: Teaching with Primary Sources in Grades 4–5*, Monica Edinger, a fourth-grade teacher, testifies about the effectiveness of using primary sources with children:

> For years I've used primary sources with great success in my fourth-grade classroom to help my students see history not only as real and relevant but as fascinating and

intriguing. . . . Primary sources help my students to think hard about the past and to construct their own views of history instead of relying on the authors of textbooks and trade books to do it for them. The result is a classroom of curious, engaged, invested learners, students who are having memorable learning experiences. (Edinger 2000, 2–3)

Connecting Students with Young People Making Contributions Today

Connecting our students with young people in other places and time periods by using primary sources can empower and inspire them. So can connecting them with contemporary young people who are involved in making a better world today. When students realize that others like them, both in the past and today, have made and can make a difference, they are encouraged to become involved too. Such involvement addresses the NCSS goal of participatory citizenship and four of the performance expectations of the NCSS "Civic Ideals and Practice" theme:

> [T]he learner can . . . locate, access, organize, and apply information about an issue of public concern from multiple points of view; identify and practice selected forms of civic discussion and participation . . . ; explain actions citizens can take to influence public policy decisions; and recognize and interpret how the "common good" can be strengthened through various forms of citizen action. (NCSS 1994, 73)

I am amazed by stories of children being empowered for civic participation by other children. Recently I read *Iqbal Masih and the Crusaders Against Child Slavery,* by Susan Kuklin. It is the story of a boy, born in Pakistan in 1982, who became a debt-bonded laborer at age four. He wove carpets twelve hours a day, sometimes chained to the loom. When he was ten, Iqbal slipped away from work to go to a meeting of the Bonded Labor Liberation Front, where he found help to become free and to go to school. But that was not enough: Iqbal had to help others be free, too. His crusade eventually led him to America, where he spoke to students about working against child labor and where he received the Reebok Human Rights Youth in Action Award. In his award acceptance speech, Iqbal said,

> I am one of those millions of children who are suffering in Pakistan because of bonded labor and child labor. . . . Unfortunately, the owner of the business where I worked told us that it is America who asks us to enslave the children. American people like the cheap carpets, the rugs, and the towels that we make. (Kuklin 1998, 3)

Students at a middle school in Massachusetts were so inspired by Iqbal's visit to their school that they got 656 letters from their neighborhood protesting child bondage. Amanda Loos, a student at Broad Meadows School in Quincy, Massachusetts, wrote,

When Iqbal spoke to us, he made me look at what I had differently. He showed me that it was wrong to take things for granted and that it was important to speak against things that were wrong. I thought, if Iqbal could make a difference, so could I. (75)

Sadly, when Iqbal returned home to Pakistan, the death threats that had been made against him by the carpet producers came true. Although he lived only twelve years, Iqbal's crusade continues to live on through the work of other young people.

Children today. Children in the past. Our students need to "meet" them, to be inspired and empowered by them. Yes, they need to know about the accomplishments of adults like Martin Luther King Jr., Eleanor Roosevelt, and Abraham Lincoln. But they also need to know what people near their age have done and are doing.

History tells us who we were, who we are, and who we can become. Keith Barton and Linda Levstik, who have done extensive research on teaching history to children, emphasize the "becoming":

> Because history is a work in progress, it always tells us more than who we were or who are at the moment. By marking our particular paths to the present, history also points to some possible paths to the future and forecloses others. . . . Students who do not see themselves as members of groups who had agency in the past or power in the present, who are invisible in history, lack viable models for the future. (Levstik and Barton 1997, 2)

They give an example of traditional history instruction emphasizing the achievements of the men who settled the West while presenting women as simply having followed their husbands. I would add that, although traditional instruction presents women as having been present in a passive way, it presents children as almost invisible.

Getting Acquainted with the Resources

Teachers can integrate the study of children into most social studies themes, topics, or periods of history. Many excellent resources have primary sources that are suitable for use with children; these can be supplemented with secondary sources if needed.

A good way to begin is to become acquainted with some classic sources of information about young people in history and today. These are my favorites— the ones I depend on and use most often. The most recent and perhaps the most complete book on children in history that I know of is one I had been hoping that someone would write: Phillip Hoose's *We Were There, Too! Young People in U.S. History* (2001). One of the best sources for stories of children who are activists today is Hoose's *It's Our World, Too! Stories of Young People Who Are Making a Difference* (1993). If you can get only a few books, start with these.

Two complete issues of *Cobblestone* are dedicated to children in history (January 1989, "Children Who Shaped History") and children as activists (December 1993, "Kid Power: Changing Public Policy"). Jackdaw's collections of primary source photographs include sets that show young people in history. Russell Freedman has written a number of books that fascinate children, including *Immigrant Kids* (1992) and *Children of the Wild West* (1983). The Blue Earth Books series Diaries, Letters, and Memoirs feature children's diary entries from different historical periods. All of these resources are excellent and readily available, but they are only the beginning. I have enjoyed locating and collecting an extensive number of other resources, and I'm still searching. Once you and your students share the excitement of discovering new resources, you may not be able to stop searching either!

Using the Resources

Teachers know that having access to the right resources is only one piece of a program. Integrating those resources into the existing curriculum using teaching methods and strategies that are grounded in theory and research is the other big piece. What do you do with your resources? How do you use them?

I decide how to use resources based primarily on the theory of constructivism, which has its roots in the work of Vygotsky and Piaget. I refer to recent research on teaching children history by Linda Levstik and Keith Barton (1997), Jere Brophy and Bruce VanSledright (1997), and other social studies researchers. I take into account the cultural diversity in classrooms and students' backgrounds, ways of communicating, and learning styles. I consult books and articles in which teachers such as Monica Edinger or Tarry Lindquist describe their best practices. I draw on the most effective social studies teaching that I have seen or experienced. Finally, I use the NCSS standards as a guide. In each of these decisions the emphasis is on students "doing" social studies—not just learning isolated facts.

Constructivism is the view that students construct knowledge based on their own experiences and on their prior knowledge. Social interaction facilitates this construction. In describing the characteristics of constructivism, Paul Eggen and Don Kauchak state that learners do not record copies of what they read or hear like a tape recorder. Instead, "they interpret stimuli on the basis of what they know, and they construct understanding that makes sense to them" (2001, 294). The NCSS Task Force on Standards for Teaching and Learning in the Social Studies believes that this active construction of knowledge is one of the key features of powerful social studies teaching and learning. Students construct knowledge when they engage in inquiry, discovery, experimentation, and meaningful, authentic activities that are similar to the ones they encounter in the outside world.

The resources by and about young people described in this book can be used most effectively when they are incorporated into ongoing study that gives students time to immerse themselves in a historical period. This kind of in-depth instruction means that teachers may not cover as much content during the school year, but as research shows,

> Understanding complicated concepts . . . develop gradually over time; students learn more each time they encounter them. In-depth understanding also requires the time for sustained attention: students have to study topics in enough depth to understand them and to reflect on the meaning and significance of what they've studied. (Levstik and Barton 1997, 11)

When we attempt to get through a social studies textbook by the end of the school year, we may be covering a lot of information, but it's unlikely that students spend much time engaged in meaningful learning. How many of us have had the same experience as this fifth-grade teacher:

> You have to go into a topic in depth, not just see who can get to the American Revolution by May; otherwise, they won't remember it. I may be slow because I'm just on Jamestown, but my students still remember what they learned about Native Americans. It's important that they're actually *doing* history, not just memorizing information. (Levstik and Barton 1997, 10)

When students have the opportunity for in-depth study, they can develop questions, collect information, make interpretations, and explain—for example—the impact of the Industrial Revolution on families, or the issues involved in the civil rights movement. They can absorb enough about a time period and its events and people to imagine themselves in the situations of the children who lived then, so they can complete activities from the perspective of historical young people such as by writing a journal in the voice of a pioneer child or role-playing young people involved in a Lowell mill strike. This book describes many such activities and includes ideas for problem solving, such as deciding whether to risk helping slaves escape on the Underground Railroad or to hide Jewish children during World War II.

Understanding the perspectives of other children can help students work through events in their own lives and cope with what may be similar situations. For example, Deborah Cox writes about her fifth graders' study of the antebellum South. Because her students seemed to "understand others best in terms of themselves" (2000, 17), she provided information from the perspectives of children who lived in towns, the backwoods, and on plantations, particularly in relation to education, leisure time, work, and family. Cox then had the students write fictional stories based on their interpretations of life back then. After reading excerpts from *Incidents in the Life of a Slave Girl*, by Harriet Jacobs, one African American student wrote about the separation of a slave from his parents when they were sold. The boy later became reunited with his family, and they all lived happily every after. The present-day meaning for this student was that he was living with one parent and had recently met his older brother for the first time. He stated that "some of my family was slave I think." According to Cox, this student

> seems to project his own joy at meeting his older brother onto the slave family's reunion. . . . Thus within this historical scenario, [the student] was able to create a story of significance to himself both personally and historically. He imagines that his feelings and experiences are not that different from those of people in the past. (18)

Our students can make connections with history when it is approached as narrative—as true stories about real people. They have highly developed schema and networks of information about the people and stories that have been part of their life experiences. Using methods that emphasize narrative and the human side of social studies engages students emotionally and enables them to make their own connections with history. When they hear or read narratives about young people like them who experienced and made decisions about events in the past, they can make a leap from the past to their lives today.

Jere Brophy and Bruce VanSledright (1997) emphasize that personalizing historical content is an effective way to help students understand history. In referring to theory and research about teaching history "(Barton and Levstik, 1996; Knight, 1993; Levstik and Barton, 1996; Low-Beer and Blyth, 1983; Willig, 1990)" (1997, 262), they state that one set of widely recommended principles calls for studying individuals or groups of people in a way that allows students to develop empathy with the people they're studying and to understand the context in which those people lived. Brophy and VanSledright suggest using narrative content that portrays people with whom students can identify.

When I attended a National Council of Social Studies conference recently, I saw this African proverb featured at an exhibit:

> No people should be starving for their own image.

By connecting our students with children in the past and present, we enable them to find their own image in others. We empower them to create their own history today.

Looking Ahead

In the following chapters I share resources and methods for connecting social studies students with other children, historical and present-day. Each chapter is built around a theme or period of history that's commonly studied in elementary and middle grades. I describe real children of that period or related to that topic and introduce resources about them, then explain and illustrate ways of using those primary sources. Each chapter also has a section that describes how young people today are creating their own histories by making contributions for a better world. Finally, I give ideas and suggestions about how the students in your classrooms can take action today.

For example, in the chapter titled "Children in Slavery, Children Laboring and Striking," I begin with stories and pictures of children who were slaves and who worked in unsafe conditions in mills, coal mines, glass factories, canneries, and sweat shops during the Industrial Revolution. Specific children are featured, such as young Frederick Douglass, who taught himself to read in spite of efforts to keep slaves from reading, or Harriet Hanson, an eleven-year-old Lowell mill worker who helped lead a strike. Next, suggestions are given for introducing students to the young people featured in the chapter. Activities such as reenacting a strike at Lowell are described to help students try to experience what their lives were like. Information is then given about children today who labor in terrible conditions in third world countries and about children like Iqbal Masih and other young crusaders against child slavery. Finally, ideas are shared on how your students, inspired by these historical and contemporary role models, can take action today by working to persuade people to stop buying from companies who use child labor. In each of the next five chapters, I follow this pattern of introducing young people past and present, sharing ideas for using resources about them in the classroom, and offering suggestions for engaging students in their own contributions today.

Throughout the book I use terms and phrases such as *children, young people,* and *people near our students' age* interchangeably to mean anyone from early childhood through the young teen years. Most of the references at the end of the book include a brief description to help you determine whether you might want to use a resource with your students.

Now I invite you to join me as we meet young people in the past and present who can motivate your students to engage in historical inquiry and inspire them to make their own contributions for a better world.

2

Children Moving, Children Settling

Our family . . . left this morning for . . . California. My father started our wagons one month in advance, to St. Joseph, Missouri, our starting point. . . . The last hours were spent in bidding good bye to old friends. My mother is heartbroken. . . . The last good bye has been said—the last glimpse of our old home on the hill, and a wave of the hand . . . to kind teachers and schoolmates, and we are off.

SALLIE HESTER, *who moved to California in 1849, when she was fourteen*
(Hester 2000, 8–10)

There were no regrets on my part at leaving my relatives and my native town. It meant for me adventure.

MARTHA PLASSMAN, *who traveled at age thirteen from Ohio to Montana in 1863*
(Dean 1984, 38 in Peavy and Smith 1999, 18)

We . . . drove . . . to the ranch and a sorry looking place it was. The first look we had at it [my sister] Esther and I cried and asked Uncle to turn around and go straight back to Michigan. The house consisted of two shacks . . . and the fields were covered with stubble.

FLORENCE WEEKS, *upon arriving at her uncle's ranch in California in 1859, when she was eight*
(Weeks 1859 in Werner 1995, 152)

My first day at school was a very frightening experience. As we entered the schoolyard, several girls formed a ring around us, singing a song and dancing in a circle. . . . They ran away when a tall woman came toward us. Her bright yellow hair and big blue eyes looking down at me were a fearful sight; it was my first close look at such a person. She was welcoming me to her school, but I was frightened. When she addressed me, I answered in Korean, "I don't understand you." I turned around, ran all the way home, and hid in our shack.

MARY PIAK LEE, *born in Korea, who moved to California in 1900 at age six*
(Lee 1990, 16 in Hoobler and Hoobler 1999, 33)

I remember when we landed, squirming through all the grown-up people to see the Statue of Liberty. . . . I don't think anyone realizes the excitement of a new country.

GRETCHEN YOST, *who came to the United States from Sweden in 1919*
(Hoobler and Hoobler 1997, 43)

Moving and settling! Who among us has not relocated at least a few times in our lives? I have moved and settled six times so far. With the mobility of U.S. society, the instability of much modern family life, and the conflicts in some areas of the world today, many of our students have moved and settled, too. An event, thought, or feeling related to their moving may be similar to one of those expressed in the quotations above and in the following paragraphs. In this chapter we meet children who have moved and settled in a variety of time periods and situations. Teachers can use this common experience to help our students make a historical connection and see the relevance of history in their own lives.

Moving West

When teachers hear "moving and settling" in relation to social studies, possibly the first thing that many of us think of is the movement westward in America in the 1800s. Images of wagon trains, pioneers, hardships, dangers, the prairie, sod houses, and encounters with Native Americans may come to our minds. Children's literature on this topic includes the *Little House on the Prairie* books, which are wonderful resources to use with children, especially because Laura Ingalls Wilder actually experienced what she wrote about. Her historical fiction books are fictionalized memoirs, rather than the kind of historical fiction that's based solely on research, according to Joan Blos (Tunnell and Ammon 1985, 14–15). Blos believes that historical fiction gives students a sense of what life was like in the past, and those of us who have used Wilder's books can certainly attest to this. However, reading primary sources about real children's experiences helps prevent students from developing a distorted view of pioneer life and of the people who lived during that time, including Native Americans. Our students can identify with real children who faced and overcame hardships, especially hardships like their own. For example, as with many students today, some pioneer children did not have loving families to help them, or had lost one or both parents. Matthew Downey admits that as a fifth grader, Wilder's books may have misled him: "A young reader might well conclude . . . that frontier mothers were always loving and protective, fathers ever resourceful and competent, and children untroubled and free of self-doubt. . . . The novel does not hold up a real-life mirror to help young people see themselves more clearly" (1986, 264).

Fortunately, we do have the diaries and recollections of people who traveled and settled in the West as children. Moving for them usually meant a long and arduous journey. One of the most fascinating diaries I have read was written by Ada Millington, a twelve-year-old who wrote almost every day in 1862 as she made the trip from Keosauqua, Iowa, to Santa Rosa, California. What makes Ada's diary so interesting to students is her ability to describe in detail what she saw, the diversity of the people she met, the situations her group encountered in getting their wagons to California, and her own reactions to all of this.

I always enjoy learning about other teachers' "best practices" and what works well for them in the classroom, especially teachers who use young peoples' diaries and letters. Lillian Valle-Condell and Karen Gordon (1986) wrote about how their students made connections with Ada Millington as they read her diary. I am fascinated by the diary's effect on the refugee children in Lillian's fifth-grade classroom who had recently arrived from Southeast Asia. Ada wrote in 1862 about the animals used in the wagon train:

> Wednesday, May 7. . . . We forded Grand River and had a steep hill to ascend immediately after crossing. Our ox, old "Selim," stumbled and came near to getting severly lamed. We saw much excellent prairie, rolling and covered with luxuriant grass. (Millington 1977, 26)
>
> Monday, May 12. . . . One of Uncle Michael's oxen refused to cross the bridge over the Tarkio (River) and the men finally had to tie a rope around his horns and hitch a yoke of cattle to him and pull him across. When he saw he was bound to go, he concluded he wanted to go, but they jerked him along so fast, he had to scramble to keep on his feet. (27)

When the class discussed the animals, a girl from Vietnam said that the water buffalo in her country were similar to oxen. Some Laotian students explained that rice farmers in Laos use water buffalo to plow their fields. The Southeast Asian students then conducted research comparing water buffalo and oxen. Lillian writes, "I was delighted to see these otherwise reticent students become so animated when the subject focused on their homeland and its culture" (Valle-Condell and Gordon 1986, 277).

One of the preservice teachers in my social studies methods course encountered an interesting situation when she first presented Ada's diary to the fourth-grade class she was teaching. Some students had trouble believing that the diary was really written by someone who lived so long ago. Our methods class decided that the students would be helped by seeing copies of pages from the original diary, in Ada's own handwriting. After learning from this experience, I began to collect copies of pages from original diaries, in addition to transcripts. The first I collected were from the diary of Barsina Rogers French, who at thirteen traveled with her family through the Arizona Territory in 1867 (Figure 2–1). These pages reveal that Barsina was just as careful as Ada in recording the details of her trip. Students would find it interesting to see what her actual diary looked like and to read her accounts in her own handwriting. (Some parts of historical diaries may be faded and difficult to read. Your students might enjoy using a magnifying glass as they try to figure out words that aren't clear—just like detectives searching for historical clues.)

Tragedies and losses, as well as children's chores, responsibilities, and diversions, are recorded in young people's diaries. Sallie Hester, who journeyed as a

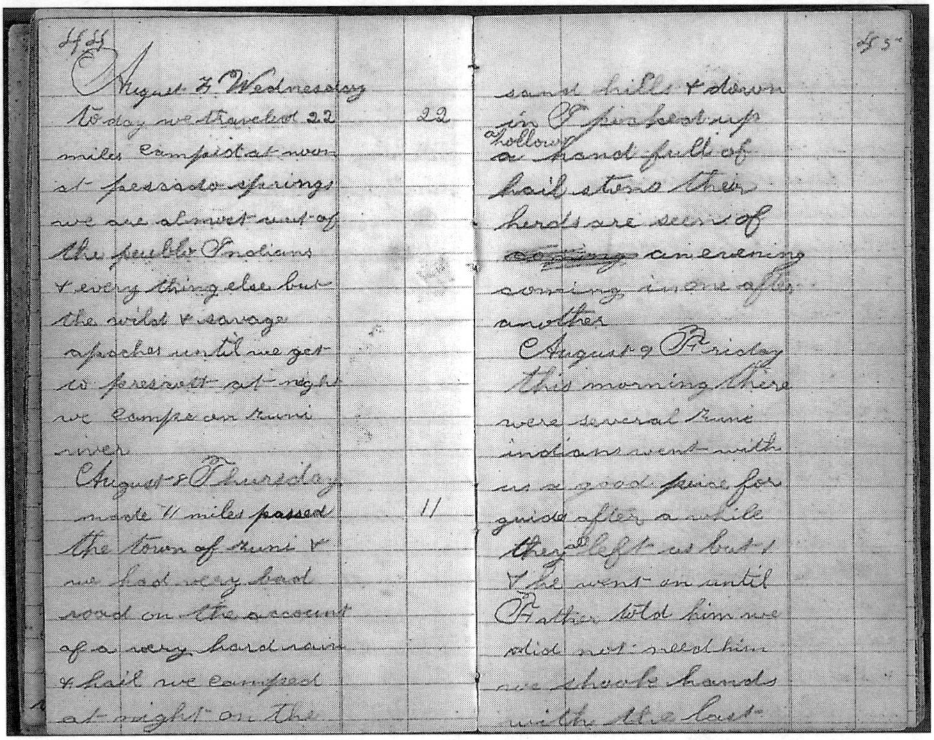
August 7 Wednesday
To day we traveled 22 miles campeist at noon at pessado springs we are almost out of the pueblo Indians & every thing else but the wild & savage apaches until we get to prescott at night we camped on zuni river
August 8 Thursday
made 11 miles passed the town of zuni & we had very bad road on the account of a very hard rain & hail we camped at night on the

sand hills & down in P picked up a hand full of hollow hail stone their herds are seen of an evening coming in one after another
August 9 Friday
This morning there were several zuni indians went with us a good piece for guide after a while they left us but 1 & he went on until Father told him we did not need him we shook hands with the last

Figure 2–1. Pages from the 1867 diary of Barsina Rogers French (courtesy of the Huntington Library, San Marino, California). *Continued on next page.*

38

July 25 Thursday
this morning we set-
out over the prarie
out of any road
set out west to
try & make it to
water as quick as
possible after a
little while we
came to the rio
puerco a little nasty
river after a little
while a mexican
came along & told
us that we were 2
miles above the
road this evening
we drove down to
the road

39

15°

July 26 Friday
made 15 miles
camped for noon at
Sheep springs at first
we could not find
any water but
mother went up
the cannion & she
found some water
& then father went
& found some pools
of water at night
we camped at a
little pond of
water where
there were some very
good grass
July 27 Saturday
we passed Elrita
& also Lesguna San

32

traveled all night
to make it to
water in good
time to water in
the morning made
80 miles & the
mules & horses were
so near give out
that we had to
stop
July 18 Thursday
this morning we
gave our horses a
little water &
started on we
drove about 20 miles   20
& found some water
& stopped for night
the mexican left
us tonight

33

July 19 Friday
passed tagari up
in the cannion
we drove out of the
cannion about 19   19
miles
July 20 Saturday
Father unloaded 1
of the wagons &
went into Albegurque
July 21 Sunday
passed Albegurke &
drove 4 miles below   14
to the ferrie across
the rio grand when
we arrived there
there was about 20
Pueblo Indians
waiting to go across
they seem to be

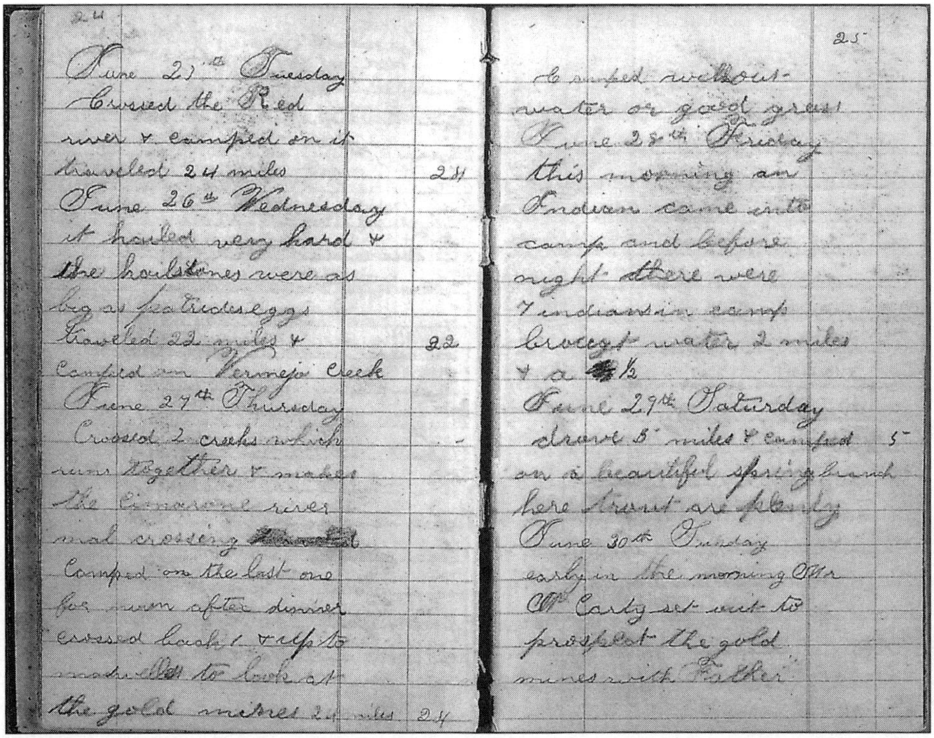

Figure 2–1. *Continued.*

fourteen-year-old in 1849, described almost drowning, seeing dead cattle, burying people who died of cholera, and struggling to cross the desert.

> September 4— . . . Stopped . . . and supplied ourselves with water for the desert. Had a trying time crossing. Several of our cattle gave out. . . . The weary journey . . . the mooing of the cattle for water . . . the cry of "Another ox down," the stopping of train to unyoke the poor dying brute, . . . the weary, weary tramp of men and beasts worn out with heat and famished for water, will never be erased from my memory. Just at dawn we had a glimpse of the Truckee River and with it the feeling: Saved at last! (Hester 2000, 22)

Portions of Sallie's diary are in *A Covered Wagon Girl: The Diary of Sallie Hester, 1849–1850*, a juvenile book that includes background information and ideas for activities such as making dried apples, which the pioneers ate, and keeping a diary. Although the family shown in Figure 2–2 is not from Sallie's wagon train, students could easily imagine her or Ada in this scene, resting after a full day's travel.

Children who traveled west discovered the opportunity to take on different roles than they would have back home. For example, eleven-year-old Mary Ellen Todd drove the oxen pulling her family's wagon to Oregon:

> How my heart bounded . . . when I chanced to hear father say to mother, "Do you know that Mary Ellen is beginning to crack the whip?" Then how it fell again, when mother replied, "I am afraid it isn't a very lady-like thing for a girl to do." After this, while I felt a secret joy in being able to have power that sets things going, there was also some sense of shame. (West 1985, 94)

Marion Russell wrote a book about her trip as a seven-year-old in 1852. Ginger Wadsworth's *Along the Santa Fe Trail: Marion Russell's Own Story* was adapted for children from Russell's diary; it has beautiful watercolor paintings. Marion wrote of the wonders and difficulties of traveling in a wagon train with her mother and brother after her stepfather died. Selections from her autobiography, *Land of Enchantment: Memoirs of Marion Russell Along the Santa Fe Trail*, could be read by older students to provide greater depth.

When the traveling children arrived at their families' destinations, their reactions varied. Some were disappointed because what they saw was so different from what they had known. Grace McCance Snyder wrote about arriving at the family

Figure 2–2. Pioneers resting on their journey west (courtesy of the Denver Public Library, Western History Collection, x11929).

homestead in Nebraska and seeing "soddies" (sod houses).

> I can still see the homestead as it looked when we pulled into it that day—just two naked little soddies squatting on a bare, windswept ridge. . . . Not another building in sight, not a tree, not an animal, nothing but grassy flats and hills. (Snyder 1963 in Warren 1998, 12)

This excerpt is from Andrea Warren's *Pioneer Girl: Growing Up on the Prairie*, the true story of Grace's life, which is filled with quotations from Grace's memoirs. Older students could read selections from her memoir, *No Time on My Hands*, recorded by Snyder's daughter, Nellie Snyder Yost.

Others wrote of exploring a new and interesting place or of feeling more grown-up because they found themselves being given more responsibilities. Mary Alice Zimmerman did farm chores with her father, rather than housework:

> I helped my father on the farm and learned to do the work pretty well, as I was strong for a girl. I soon preferred to have a team to myself when possible. I have always loved the great open out-of-doors, and I think that it was as much from choice as from necessity that I was much of the time out on the farm at work with father. (Stratton 1981, 145)

Through reading diaries like that of Sarah Gillespie, a twelve-year-old pioneer farm girl in Iowa, students can discover more about what day-to-day life was like for pioneer children. In 2000, this diary was published in an edited edition for children, titled *A Pioneer Farm Girl: The Diary of Sarah Gillespie, 1877–1878*. Older students could read selections from the 1993 original, *All Will Yet Be Well: The Diary of Sarah Gillespie Huftalen, 1873–1952*.

Children who settled in the West before schools were established had to make adjustments. Martha Hutchinson described her situation as not having many advantages for a twelve-year-old: There was no school and her parents could not teach her because they could not read or write. Others, like Roxanna Rice, were more fortunate:

> I remember the first school I attended. . . . I and my brother, with another boy, occupied a bench with no back near the stove. When the stove became too warm, we whirled and faced the other side. The boy with us wore a paddle fastened around his neck. On this paddle were pasted several letters of the alphabet and these were changed every day. How I envied that boy because his folks were taking so much pains with him. The attention given him I coveted, though the letters he paraded I knew as well as I do today. I do not know how I learned to read. We had the English reader and . . . Webster's great spelling book. . . . My brother, older than myself, complained one day that his lesson was hard. . . . To my surprise, I could read it without a hitch. (Stratton 1981, 159–160)

Perhaps Roxanna attended a school similar to the one in Figure 2–3 and had the prairie for a playground, like the children in Figure 2–4.

The most comprehensive book that I have found on children in the West is *Frontier Children*, by Linda Peavy and Ursula Smith (1999), which covers children's journeys westward and their lives in the West, including play, schooling, chores, and their interactions with the environment and with the people in their lives. I like the book's wealth of remarkable photographs of children, the range of primary sources printed in the text, and, most of all, the diversity. Elliott West, in the foreword to this book, praises the diversity aspect of it.

> The frontier was . . . an often chaotic mingling and collision of many peoples. Peavy and Smith bring Chinese, Hispanics, Paiutes, African Americans, Sioux, and Sheepeaters into a story too often reserved for east-to-west European Americans. (x)

Frontier Children is a wonderful resource from which teachers can select photos and quotations to use with younger students. Although it is written for adults, older students could read selected parts of the book, and they would find the photos fascinating.

Figure 2–3. Going to school in Colorado, 1887 (courtesy of the Denver Public Library, Western History Collection, X-13959).

Figure 2–4. Recess at Pine Creek School in Montana, 1898 (courtesy of the Montana Historical Society, Helena, #950–880).

Emmy Werner's *Pioneer Children on the Journey West* (1995) is another good classroom resource. Although it has few photographs, it contains an abundance of selections from children's diaries and from the memoirs of adults who were pioneer children. Chapter 10 has three complete primary sources written by children: a letter written by Mary Murphy, age thirteen, on May 25, 1847, after she lost six members of her family when the Donner party was snowbound in the mountains; the diary of Sallie Hester, age fourteen, from March 20, 1849; and a letter written by Elizabeth Keegan, age twelve, on December 12, 1852, when she arrived in California. The notes and bibliographies in Peavy and Smith's and Werner's books are valuable for teachers who want to find more primary sources.

Russell Freedman's *Children of the Wild West* (1983) is an excellent general resource for students. It includes photographs and a number of quotes from people who lived during this time. Freedman tells of children traveling west, settling and working in the West, attending frontier schools, and having fun.

The preservice teachers in my social studies methods course use Freedman's book when they teach units on the settlement of the West. One teacher combined photographs, portions of Ada's diary, and selections from Freedman's book in a lesson to help her fourth-grade students connect with pioneer children. After the students worked with these resources, she asked them to write in their journals about ways they could relate to the earlier children. The students found many commonalities, such as reading, having chores, and playing the same games:

> I can relate to them because I like to jump rope and play tag with my friends and children in the West then liked to play the same exact games, too.

One fourth-grade boy was able to link his own experience of moving to the pioneer children, who, like him, had no choice about relocating:

> I could relate with the children when I was sitting on a horse. . . . I was on a farm then . . . at my friend's farm. . . . He was in my class at my school but in the middle of the year we had to move.

Another fourth-grade student seemed a little envious when he mentioned what he would say to pioneer children: "Can you and me switch lives?"

Native American Experiences

Native American children's experiences of moving and settling were much different from those of pioneer children. Native Americans were already living in the West. Some tribes moved from summer camps to winter villages each year. Others journeyed in search of new hunting grounds. These moves were organized and relatively safe for children, compared to the pioneers' trips. Ada Millington described a scene similar to the one in Figure 2–5.

> Friday, May 30. Cloudy and cool this morning and looked much like rain. Soon after starting, we began to meet Indians who were moving eastward. We kept on meeting them until nearly noon. They had their goods packed on their ponies' backs. The tent poles were fastened to the ponies side by one end, while the other end would drag on the ground. Sometimes the squaws would ride; sometimes lead and other times, drive the ponies. (Millington 1977, 36)

Charles Eastman, known as *Hakadah* by his Sioux relatives, wrote *Indian Boyhood* about his childhood with his native tribe. His book was originally published in 1902. As I was reading it, I came across an event that occurred as his tribe was moving to a place where they could find more buffalo, because the *Washechu* (white men) were beginning to destroy the herds. On this particular day, most of the men were off hunting, leaving the women, children, and elderly to continue the trip. There was a commotion at the head of their calvacade and Charles rushed to the front, thinking they were being attacked by a hostile tribe. Instead,

Figure 2–5. Stump Horn family preparing for a trip across Montana's plains (courtesy of the Montana Historical Society, Helena, #981–030).

it was a huge grizzly bear, boldly opposing the tribe's progress. The old men finally killed the bear after courageous fighting by both bear and men. Eastman's description is so vivid that I could just see how a class of fourth graders would react to it. They would be able to imagine themselves with Hakadah, witnessing the event (Eastman, 223–225).

Eleven-year-old pioneer Elisha Brooks had an encounter with a migrating band from a friendly Crow tribe when his family was left behind by their wagon train because of problems with their wagon. The Crow traveled with Elisha's family to ensure their safety.

> "We presented a strange . . . scene . . . enroute: red men in rich robes of bear and panther skins decked out with fringe and feathers, . . . handsome squaws in elegant mantles of bird skins, tattooed and adorned with beads; . . . papooses rolled in highly ornamented cradles grinning from the backs of their ancestors; toddling papooses; . . . ponies hidden under monumental burdens; packs of dogs creeping under wonderful loads, . . ." and behind them was Elisha's family's "old ox team with six wild, ragged children and a woman [his mother] once called white and sometimes unwashed, for we could not always get water enough to drink." (Brooks 1992 in Werner 1995, 122)

Barsina Rogers French wrote about interactions with members of different tribes as she and her family traveled. In the pages from her diary shown in Figure 2–1 are accounts of Native Americans bringing water to the pioneers' camp and serving as guides.

Some pioneer children developed an appreciation for the culture of the Native Americans when members of tribes visited them. Eliza McAuley described how in 1852 a Pawnee chief and some of his braves visited her wagon train's camp and asked to stay the night. At dawn, she was awakened by the braves and their chief singing the tribe's morning song. Eliza wrote, "The old chief started the song and the others chimed in and it was very harmonious and pleasing" (McAuley 1852 in Werner 1995, 120).

The young daughter of a Sioux chief visited ten-year-old Kate McDaniel's camp in 1853. Kate described the girl's soft, white buckskin gown, with deep fringes at the bottom, and long leggings. Kate was fascinated:

> I could not keep my eyes off her. . . . The little princess, as we liked to call her, let us pet her pony and then showed us how she could ride and what her pony could do. . . . Then [she] jumped into her saddle, waved her hand to us, and with a little giggling laugh, was gone like a beautiful bird. (McDaniel 1853 in Werner 1995, 121)

Some modern-day students are surprised when they hear of these friendly encounters between pioneers and local tribes. A preservice teacher who read passages like these to her fourth-grade students reported to our social studies methods class the reaction of one student who claimed he knew a lot about Native Americans. The boy had the view that all encounters between pioneers and Native Americans were hostile, and he had difficulty integrating this new information. His view gradually changed as the teacher continued to read about positive interactions, such as this one from Ada's diary:

> Thursday, May 29. . . . About half-past eleven, we came to the Indians. There were about seven tents or wigwams. . . . The Indians were of a dull copper color, something like wet clay and had long, straight black hair. They were very friendly and want to shake hands with us. (Millington 1977, 36)

This child's reaction to what was for him new information prompted our methods class to discuss how students construct knowledge based on their prior and current understandings.

These friendly encounters between pioneers and Native Americans changed as more and more settlers came West. Sarah Winnemucca, the granddaughter of the chief of the Piutes described the changes in her tribe's relationship with white settlers. Selections from her book *Life Among the Piutes: Their Wrongs and Claims* can be used with students to help them understand this change. Sarah's people lived in almost all of what is now known as Nevada when she was a small child and the first white people came. The Piutes assisted the pioneers, but three years later they began to hear terrifying news from other tribes of whites killing everybody.

The preservice teacher who read to her fourth-grade class about friendly relations between tribes and pioneers helped her students understand the conflicts that developed as more settlers arrived. Using Russell Freedman's *Children of the Wild West* as a resource, the students discussed the situation from the points of view of both the tribes and the settlers. The teacher then had half of the class pretend to be young people belonging to different tribes and the other half pretend to be settlers. She asked each student to write to someone on the other side using a letter format and prompts she created (Figure 2–6). Most of the students' letters showed that they understood the conflict fairly well. For example, many of the students pretending to be members of a tribe wrote that they were in the West because their ancestors lived there, or because they were born there. They stated that they had the right to live where they did because they were there first or because their home was there. Some of the children pretending to be pioneers wrote that they were in the West looking for new opportunities, a nice place to settle, or a new home. They said that they had the right to be there because they needed a new place to live or a new life, because the West was where they belonged, or because "It is a free country." Students on both sides gave similar ideas for getting along, such as sharing the land, cooperating, trading, talking together, and not killing the buffalo for sport. However, others, depending on their role, said that the settlers should get out or the tribes should make room for them. The classroom teacher and the preservice teacher were pleased with the students' ability to put themselves into the role assigned.

When studying the settlement of the West, it is important to include the forced movement of the tribes to reservations and schools, which changed Native Americans' way of life forever. Children attending the schools were forced to give up their own cultures. Students can compare the photographs in Figures 2–7 and 2–8 to see how children were changed at these schools.

Russell Freedman includes these two photographs in his book *Children of the Wild West*, and two that show a group of boys on their arrival and fifteen months later. In *Get a Clue! An Introduction to Primary Sources*, JoAnne Deitch shows before-and-after photographs of boys and gives scaffolding questions to aid students in comparing them and making inferences about them.

In 1893, when he was eight years old, Lone Wolf, a Blackfoot, was taken from his parents to Fort Shaw Indian School in Montana.

> It was very cold that day when we were loaded into wagons. . . . Oh, we cried for this was the first time we were to be separated from our parents. . . . Nobody waved as

Native American/Pioneer Letter-Writing Format with Prompts

Directions: Pretend that you are a Native American or a pioneer in the West. If you are a pioneer, address your letter to a Native American young person. If you are a Native American, address your letter to a pioneer young person. Create a name for yourself and the person you are writing.

_____
Date

Dear _____,

    I am in the West because _____

_____

_____.

    I think I have the right to live here because _____

_____

_____.

    If I could change one thing about living in the West, I would _____

_____

_____.

    The settlers and the Native American people could get along better if

_____

_____.

    Thank you for listening to my point of view.

Sincerely,

_____

Figure 2–6. Native American/Pioneer Letter-Writing Format with Prompts (designed by Sally Mello).

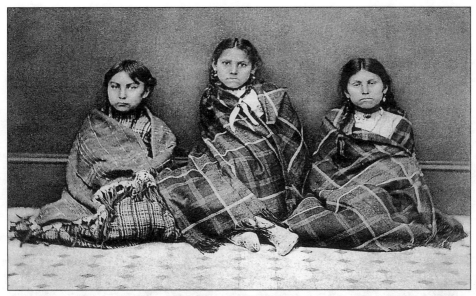

Figure 2–7. Three girls, ages ten, twelve, and thirteen, when they first arrived at Hampton Normal Agricultural Institute in 1878 (courtesy of the Smithsonian Institution, #55516).

the wagons, escorted by the soldiers, took us toward the school. . . . Once there our belongings were taken from us, even the little medicine bags our mothers had given us to protect us from harm. Everything was placed in a heap and set afire. (Dean 1984, 40, in Peavy and Smith 1999, 121)

In *We Were There, Too!*, Phillip Hoose includes the story of Chuka, a Hopi boy, whose struggle to live in two worlds began with being sent to one of these schools when he was nine. The teachers changed his name to Max, cut his hair, and took away his blanket. When Chuka returned home in the summers, his family worried that he would lose his Hopi ways. After two more years of school, he had learned to eat with a knife and fork, sleep on a bed, speak many English words, and "that a person thinks with his head instead of his heart" (Hoose 2001, 158). Teachers can select appropriate excerpts from Don Talayesva's (Chuka) autobiography, *Sun Chief: The Autobiography of a Hopi Indian*, to give students a more complete picture of his childhood, his people's way of life, and his experiences at the school the government forced him to attend.

Freedman's *Children of the Wild West* devotes a chapter to Native American children and discusses how their lives changed when they were placed on reservations or sent to government schools. Two other juvenile books, *Children of the*

Figure 2–8. The same three girls fourteen months later. Their names are listed as Annie Dawson, Carrie Anderson, and Sarah Walker (courtesy of the Smithsonian Institution, #55517).

Indian Boarding Schools, by Holly Littlefield, and *Indian School: Teaching the White Man's Way*, by Michael Cooper, are filled with photographs and contain quotes from some who attended the schools. Students can locate additional information on the following websites, which Littlefield and Cooper list:

> *http://home.epix.net/~landis/*—Stories and photographs of students who attended Carlisle Indian Industrial School in Pennsylvania, the first school built off a reservation.
>
> *http://www.hanksville.org/NAresources/indices/NAhistory.html*—An index of Native American resources on the Internet.
>
> *http://anpa.ualr.edu*—Website of the American Native Press Archives.

These resources and the photo collection *American Indians: Early Boarding Schools* by Jackdaw Publications (2001) help establish context and deepen students' understanding of the changes that Native American children faced. The photos show a variety of scenes including children arriving at the schools, attending classes, and going about daily activities. The set contains teaching ideas and background information. Using these resources can stimulate meaningful classroom discussions in which students can share their ideas and feelings about how Native American young people were forced to exchange their cultures for that of the white settlers. Students can develop empathy by describing how they would feel if they were forced into a similar situation.

Children of the Orphan Trains

Instead of traveling in wagon trains with their families, thousands of children were sent west alone by rail. Homeless children in large cities like New York and Boston were placed on trains and sent to Kansas, Missouri, Nebraska, Oklahoma, and other states by the Children's Aid Society. Almost 200,000 children traveled on these trains between 1854 and 1929. The April 1998 issue of *Cobblestone* features the orphan trains and provides background information and activities for students. Andrea Warren wrote two books about the orphan trains that include photographs, posters announcing the arrival of the trains and requesting homes for the children, and interviews of people who rode the trains. *Orphan Train Rider: One Boy's True Story* (1996) is about Lee Nailling, who boarded the train to Texas in 1926. *We Rode the Orphan Trains* (2001) includes the recollections of people who had been orphan train children. Imagine what it would be like to be placed on a train without knowing where you were going or who your new family would be!

Immigration

When you think of immigration in the late 1800s and early 1900s, what images fill your mind? The Statue of Liberty? A crowded ship? Ellis Island? Tenement housing in New York City? When I asked myself this question, I immediately visualized the two children on the cover of Russell Freedman's *Immigrant Kids* (1992). Then I began to picture other children with tired eyes, somber expressions, or questioning looks like those in Figure 2–9. We still see faces like these in our schools today among students who have recently immigrated or are refugees. From 1892 through 1954, approximately fifteen million people came to America (Fisher 1986, 8). A large percentage of these were children. The numbers now are not as high, but people continue to arrive. The children immigrating today can relate to those who came earlier because they face some of the same problems.

Primary sources by or about immigrant children are readily available for use in the classroom. *Immigrant Kids* is one of the best known. This book is filled with photographs that can be used to help students understand what moving from another country and settling in America was like for children of an earlier day. Although much of the text is secondary, the photographs and quotes make this a valuable resource. Freedman includes accounts by people arriving, going through the process at Ellis Island, adjusting to their living conditions, attending school, working, and playing.

An oral history of Elda Del Bino Willitts' journey to America is beautifully illustrated in the 2000 children's book *Journey to a New Land*, by Kimberly Weinberger. Elda was interviewed for the Ellis Island Oral History Project about her immigration from Italy and her experiences as she settled in America with her family in 1916, when she was seven years old. This is an excellent book to use with younger children because Elda's story gives a complete picture of the whole process, beginning with her family's decision to leave and continuing with her experiences aboard the ship and at Ellis Island, and what happened as she settled in California. Older students can visit the website for the Ellis Island Oral History Project, *www.i-channel.com/education/ellis/oralhist.html*, to hear interviews of other people who came over when they were children. The large photographs in the Jackdaw Publications collection *Ellis Island: the Immigrant's Experience* (1997) can be displayed around the classroom to immerse students in the immigrant experience. This photo collection includes background information, a photo analysis sheet to use with students, and ideas for activities using the photos.

One of the most complete resources for older students on this subject is the American Family Albums series published by Oxford University Press, which includes *The Chinese American Family Album*, *The Italian American Family Album*, *The Mexican American Family Album*, *The Scandinavian American Family Album*,

Figure 2–9. Family immigrating from Italy (courtesy of the Library of Congress, LCUSZ62–67910).

The African American Family Album, and others, all by Dorothy Hoobler and Thomas Hoobler. These contain period photographs and selections from letters, memoirs, and diaries that describe the "old country," the trip, and the lives and contributions of these people. Each book has writings by children or memoirs of people recalling their childhood experiences. Lily describes her experiences in the Italian album:

I came to America . . . when I was four years old. . . . In 1913. . . . We didn't speak a word of English. . . . We went to grammar school in Bayonne [New Jersey]. . . . My only problem was that while in America my mother had a new baby every two years. And I had to stay home to help take care of the babies so that my mother could scrub clothes by hand. I missed a lot of school. . . . Missing two or three days a week of school, I couldn't catch up with the work. In those days, they didn't believe a girl needed an education, because she got married and became a mother and a house-wife. All my brothers got an education and so did my two younger sisters. . . . Since I was the oldest of the girls, there was no education for me. (Hoobler and Hoobler 1994b, 87)

Reading about experiences like Lily's can stimulate discussion about how the education of girls and girls' roles were viewed then compared with how they're viewed today.

Sources about modern-day immigrant children help students understand that immigration is not just a part of our history. In *Quilted Landscape: Conversations with Young Immigrants,* by Yale Strom (1996), students can read what young people ages ten to seventeen say about immigrating and their lives in America. They will meet ten-year-old Carlos Nunez, who was born in Mukacheva, Ukraine, and now lives in Sarasota, Florida, and twelve-year-old Coreen Chand, who was born in Suva, Fiji, and lives in south San Francisco. *Dancing to America,* by Ann Morris (1994), and *Where the River Runs: A Portrait of a Refugee Family,* by Nancy Graff (1993), give students in-depth meetings with contemporary immigrants. The first is about Anton Pankevich, who enrolled in ballet school in New York after his family immigrated from Russia. Graff's book is the story of a family with three young boys who moved from Cambodia to Boston. The *Cobblestone* theme pack on immigration includes nine issues of *Cobblestone* and a teacher's guide. Some of the issues feature children, including more contemporary ones such as Alla Pruzhansky, who writes about immigrating from Russia with her family in 1980, when she was eleven.

Children in Migrant Families

Children suffered hardships when their families' economic situations were affected by the Great Depression and the dust bowl. Farm families were forced off the land and became migrant workers. Cesar Chavez told Studs Terkel how insecure he felt about losing the family farm:

Oh, I remember having to move out of our house. . . . My daddy used to do all his work with horses, so this huge tractor came in and began to knock down his corral, this small corral where my father kept his horses. We didn't understand why. In the matter of a week, the whole face of the land was changed. . . . We all of us climbed into an old Chevy my dad had. And then we were in California, and migratory workers. . . . It must have been around '36. I was about eight. Well, it was a strange life. We had been poor, but we knew every night there was a bed there, and that this was our room. It was sort of a settled life, and we had chickens and hogs, eggs, and all those things. But that all of a sudden changed. (Terkel 1970, 53–54 in King 1997, 36)

In *Children of the Dust Bowl: The True Story of the School at Weedpatch Camp* (1992), Jerry Stanley describes the "Okie" migration to California, the squalor of the squatter camps where families lived, and the hostility of local people toward them. He gives a moving account of how Leo Hart, a school superintendent, involved children in building a school just for them. The children grew crops on the school field and raised livestock. *Children of the Dust Days*, by Karen Coombs (2000), consists of children's photographs and a simple text on the history of the dust bowl; it can be used with younger students.

First Lady Eleanor Roosevelt received many letters from young people during the depression. She was an advocate for youth, and they knew it. Their letters reflect the belief that they could confide in her and perhaps obtain help. Reading some of these very personal letters requesting food, clothes, and a way out of very desperate situations will give modern-day students a sense of what uprooted children's lives were like during this period of history. I was deeply touched by their troubles and by their ability to write to a president's wife as if she were someone they knew personally. The following excerpt from a letter written in 1935 by a fourteen-year-old boy is an example of how young people confided in Mrs. Roosevelt:

I was doctering for a while without my mother and dad knowing it yet and I owe Dr. Forney $7.50. I haven't any idea how to earn this amount. I was doctering for an infected arm. Every time I went the Dr. charged $1.50 . . . right this minute I crying because I can't earn it. I don't want my parents to find [out]. (Cohen 1996, 272)

Children's letters to Mrs. Roosevelt are in the Material Assistance Requested files in the Eleanor Roosevelt papers in the Franklin D. Roosevelt Library. The children who wrote the letters are wonderful models for modern-day students as they write to public leaders about the needs of people today!

The lives of today's Mexican migrant farmworkers and their children involve constant moving and settling. *The Mexican American Family Album* (Hoobler and Hoobler 1994e) includes recollections of such lives. Larry Brimmer's book *A Migrant Family* (1991) gives students an idea of what day-to-day life is like for twelve-year-old Juan Medina, a migrant child living in a camp near San Diego,

California. One of the most moving juvenile books I have read is Beth Atkin's *Voices from the Fields: Children of Migrant Farmworkers Tell Their Stories* (1993). Although their lives are heartbreaking, their stories, poems, and photographs demonstrate resilience and hope for a better life.

Whether struggling through the desert on the journey west, facing the unfamiliar government Indian schools, or leaving their countries for America, many of the children mentioned in this chapter demonstrated the same resilience and hope. The encouragement that one small traveler offered her little brother as they stumbled wearily along the Lassen Trail in the High Sierras is reflective of the outlook of many of these children:

> Never mind, Buddy, taint far to grass and water.
>
> *Recorded by J. Goldsborough Bruff, who was also on the trail*
> *(Reed 1944, 23 in Peavy and Smith 1999, 30)*

Using the Resources

The accounts of children who moved to and settled in new areas can fit into a number of topics, themes, or content areas in social studies. A natural way to connect contemporary students' lives with the children in historical sources is to invite students to describe their own experiences in moving with their families: How did they feel about the move? What difficulties and adjustments did they face? What did they like and dislike about the move? Students can also share how they traveled and how much time their moves took. Primary sources can then be introduced, allowing students to connect their experiences with the earlier children's.

Engaging in Inquiry

Because of the variety and availability of primary sources by and about children, inquiry is an appropriate model to use with sources related to immigration or the movement west. Students can themselves "be historians" by using the resources of professional historians. Inquiry typically requires considering a problem, hypothesizing, collecting and analyzing information, and forming conclusions. Through engaging in inquiry, students develop skill in solving problems and using critical thinking. John Dewey and Jerome Bruner both called for using inquiry in teaching social studies. "Bruner thought that children should solve problems the same way as real-life social scientists and become child versions of anthropologists, sociologists, economists, and historians" (Zarrillo 2000, 121). Linda Levstik and Keith Barton (1997), who have conducted extensive research on children's understanding of history, affirm the value of inquiry:

To get more from history than preparation for a game show, students must take part in disciplined inquiry, not just repeat isolated trivia. The study of history must begin with the concerns and interests of students, and help them find answers. This means that students have to learn what it means to ask and answer historical questions—how to find information, how to evaluate sources, how to reconcile conflicting accounts, and how to create an interpretive account. (14)

Properly designed inquiry activities that use primary sources as data enable students to move toward meeting a number of National Council for the Social Studies (NCSS) standards:

- compare and contrast different stories or accounts about past events, people, places, or situations, identifying how they contribute to our understanding of the past;
- identify and use various sources for reconstructing the past, such as . . . letters, diaries, . . . photos . . . ;
- demonstrate an understanding that people in different times and places view the world differently. (NCSS 1994, 34)

Teachers would be applying the NCSS principle "Social studies teaching and learning are powerful when they are challenging" through modeling a "thoughtful approach to inquiry" and using methods "designed to elicit and support similar qualities from students" (NCSS 1994, 12).

For inquiry to work well, students must have motivating questions or problems to investigate. These can be presented by the teacher, generated by the students, or developed jointly by both teacher and students. Posing questions and problems can give students a sense of ownership and excitement. However, sometimes a lot of the questions students submit are simply factual. Students need scaffolding in developing substantial questions that are not easily solved. They can select a problem or question by asking themselves the following: Is there more than one answer to my question? Are several resources needed to answer or solve it? Have I considered asking why or how? Is it open-ended? Does it require compiling information from different sources to draw conclusions, find patterns, or make comparisons?

Here are some problems and questions that students might investigate in an inquiry using resources related to the movement west. Some are more suitable for younger students and some would work best with older students.

- How were the experiences of two or three pioneer children traveling west similar and different? (For example, students could compare and contrast the diary entries of Barsina Rogers French and Ada Millington.)

- How were pioneer children's experiences similar to and different from what you would experience if you traveled the same route today?
- How were the Native American children who were sent to government schools affected by their experiences there? How were they changed?
- How did the land and the weather affect pioneer children's trips west?
- How did pioneer children react to and interact with the Native American people they met as they traveled?
- What hardships did pioneer children experience and how did they over-come those hardships?
- How did pioneer children help their families and others as they traveled?
- What did pioneer children do for fun?
- How did pioneer children solve problems they encountered or help others solve problems?
- How did most of the pioneer children feel about the trip west?
- What effects did the trip and settling in the West have on pioneer children?
- How did the experiences of the early pioneer children differ from the experiences of those who traveled later?
- In what ways were pioneer children's lives changed by their journey and new homes? Why?

Students conducting inquiries using resources on immigration can investigate similar questions. They can examine accounts by and interviews with people who immigrated as children to learn what their lives were like in their new homes, schools, and communities. Students can compare the experiences of children who came to America in the late 1800s and early 1900s with those who arrived in the late 1900s and on to the present. Immigrant children's reactions to what they experienced and the responsibilities they had to assume can also be explored.

Problems for inquiry can be introduced by presenting contradictions. For example, you might read a paragraph from a diary in which a pioneer child expresses excitement about the beauty of the environment and the discovery of different animals, then read a paragraph from a different diary in which the writer describes hardships and misery. Ask your students which they think is more typical, then have them begin their inquiry by comparing the recollections or diaries of a variety of people. You can do the same kind of thing with photographs or paintings: Show your students a painting or sketch of settlers and Native Americans in con-flict, then contrast it with an illustration showing them interacting in a friendly way. Again, ask the students which scene is more like what most of the pioneer children who traveled before there were many settlers would have experienced.

After students decide on questions to investigate, they give their best guesses. Then they begin examining the primary sources. Other questions may arise out of their research. Record all of their questions and hypotheses on large sheets of newsprint and display them in the classroom for students to refer to as they do their research. When you introduce primary sources, students need guidance in how to use them and how to keep track of what they find. Information collection charts like those in Figures 2–10 and 2–11 will help students record what they find, make comparisons, and find patterns. Once students summarize findings and form conclusions, decisions can be made about how to share the information with classmates.

Collecting Primary Sources

Students can be involved in adding to the teacher's collection of primary sources on immigration. Going online and searching websites like the Ellis Island Oral History Project and the Library of Congress American Memory site is one way. Some students may wish to work in groups on their own oral history projects. They can interview people in their community or family members who immigrated when they were children, or invite them to class to share their experiences. Such interviews are a meaningful experience for students of any age, as well as for those being interviewed. I will never forget the time one of my college students brought her grandmother to our class to talk about her early years in Providence, Rhode Island, after emigrating from Italy. We felt as if we traveled back in time with her as she shared personal experiences and showed photos. The students asked numerous questions, and the grandmother seemed to be so pleased to be a part of her granddaughter's class. One way to locate people to interview is to contact religious and ethnic groups in the community, such as the local branch of Catholic Charities, the Jewish Federation, or the Greek Orthodox Church.

Students who have not had experience in interviewing will need practice and guidance before actually conducting an interview. M. Gail Hickey gives suggestions for using oral history technique and the interview process in the introduction to her book *Bringing History Home* (1999). James Zarrillo offers similar guidelines in his book *Teaching Elementary Social Studies* (2000). Hickey suggests having students interview in teams of two or three. I find it helpful for students to have a sheet with steps similar to the following so that they can check off each step as they complete it:

1. Describe the focus of your interview.
2. Do some background research about the time period or event related to this interview.
3. Choose the person or people you wish to interview and have your teacher or a parent make the arrangements. If the interview is not at school, your parent must be present.

Chart for Recording Findings from Diaries About Pioneer Children's Experiences		
Barsina Rogers French 1867	Sally Hester 1849–1850	Ada Millington 1862
Difficulties Traveling		
Weather		
Scenery		
Animals		
Food		
Camp Life		
Encounters with Native Americans		
Encounters with Other Pioneers		
Chores and Responsibilities		
Other Experiences		

Figure 2–10. Chart for Recording Findings from Diaries About Pioneer Children's Experiences.

	Children Arriving Late 1800s–Early 1900s	Children Arriving Late 1900s–Present
Chart for Comparing the Experiences of Children Who Immigrated from the Late 1800s to the Early 1900s and Children Who Immigrated from the Late 1900s to the Present		
Home Countries		
Difficulties Entering the United States		
Places Settled		
What Their Homes Were/Are Like		
Jobs and Responsibilities		
School Experiences		
What They Did/Do for Fun		
Difficulties Adjusting to the New Country		

Figure 2–11. Chart for Comparing the Experiences of Children Who Immigrated from the Late 1800s to the Early 1900s and Children Who Immigrated from the Late 1900s to the Present.

4. Plan questions to ask. Try to think of questions that are open-ended, such as ones beginning with "Tell me about," or "What do you remember about," or that invite the person being interviewed to recall his or her experiences: What did she do? How did he feel? What did she see and hear?
5. Practice using a tape recorder and interviewing other students in your class. Practice asking follow-up questions after you hear an answer.
6. Get a release form from your teacher and have each person you interview sign a copy. This form gives permission for you to share the information the person gives you during your interview.
7. Prepare to share the information from your interview with the class.
8. Compare what you found out in your interview with what your classmates learned from their interviews.

Oral history projects are valuable for several reasons. Students experience "being historians" as they create their own primary sources and reconstruct the past, and they use processes mentioned in the 1994 NCSS standards. They build skills in listening, reading, asking questions, observing, writing, deciding what is relevant or irrelevant and what is fact or opinion, and analyzing and organizing information. Welton (2002) mentions that "oral history activities may lead students to a better understanding and appreciation of the older generation" (377). All of these benefits make it worth the effort involved in helping students find people to interview, guiding them in learning how to interview, and arranging to transcribe their tape-recorded interviews to use as classroom resources.

Another way students can be involved in collecting primary sources by or about children who immigrated is to work with knowledgeable reference librarians in your school library and in the children's sections of public libraries. I am always amazed at how willing librarians are to spend time with me to find just the right primary source, or book that includes primary sources. Students and teachers might enjoy going on a library research quest together.

In my own searching for primary sources by or about children, I use typical research methodology, but I've discovered that it's also helpful to look through the notes, references, and bibliographies in juvenile and adult books on children in history, such as those by Phillip Hoose, Linda Peavy and Ursula Smith, Emmy Werner, and Elliot West. Our students can do this too. For example, if they are reading *Pioneer Girl: Growing Up on the Prairie* (Warren 1998), they may want to discover more of what Grace McCance Snyder has said about her life. Looking at the sources in the back of the book, they will find a listing for her autobiography, *No Time on My Hands*, which they can then request through the local library system. When I looked at the sources in Werner (1995) and Peavy and Smith

(1999), I was fascinated by how many diaries and memoirs are listed, a number of them in manuscript form. I could hardly wait to locate them. Imagine how interesting it is for a student to look at a copy of an original journal entry in a child's own handwriting! Some students are intrigued by the quality of the handwriting, the unique spelling and grammar, and the phrases and expressions used by the children of the 1800s.

Both younger and older students can look for photographs that help answer their inquiry questions. Good sources include Peavy and Smith's *Frontier Children*, the Jackdaw photo collections, Russell Freedman's *Children of the Wild West* and *Immigrant Kids*, and Carolrhoda's Picture the American Past series. Students doing an inquiry on the hardships and adjustments experienced by immigrant children, for example, could examine pictures taken on board ships, at Ellis Island, and in tenement housing. Photo analysis sheets like those in Cobblestone's Teaching with Primary Sources series, Jackdaw photo collections, and JoAnne Deitch's *Get a Clue!* (2001) are helpful in studying photographs.

Working in Groups

Working in groups as they use diaries, memoirs, and photographs for inquiry enables students to share each other's insights. Groups can be heterogeneous or formed according to students' interests. Lev Vygotsky's theories (1978) emphasize the value of social interaction in the learning process. He believed that when students cooperate and interact, certain internal developmental processes occur. When students work in groups to examine resources that reflect different perspectives and views, they also experience the advantages of hearing their classmates' interpretations and of learning from each other.

There are a number of ways that students can use resources in groups. For example, in the analyzing information step of the inquiry process, each group of students might select a different question. One group might search for information on problems pioneer children encountered and how they were solved. Another group might look for pioneer children's responsibilities and chores. A third group could find descriptions of scenery and animals, and a fourth might look into what the children did for diversion and fun. Each group would record and share its findings, then all the results would be combined in a class book, on a display, or in whatever way the class decided.

When students have had little or no experience using primary sources in inquiry, it is helpful to have them work in small groups. I have also found that using photographs is a good way to begin. For example, suppose one inquiry question was about how pioneer children's lives were similar to and different from students' lives today. After the students list their hypotheses or best guesses on large sheets of newsprint and post them, introduce the idea of using photography to gather information. Use the overhead projector to show a transparency of a photograph of pioneer children and modeling strategies for studying photographs. Ask the students to list what they see in the photograph, then show them how to do a closer examination by looking at only one section at a time, covering up the rest of the photo. After they have looked at each part, the students add to the list of what they observed. Finally, ask the students to discuss what the photograph tells them about pioneer children.

Then give each small group of students a different photograph and a record sheet for writing down information. A Venn diagram might be appropriate, with the heading "Pioneer Children" above one circle, "Our Lives Today" above the other circle, and "Similarities" above the intersection. Each group writes the title of its photo on the record sheet and begins. For example, a group that had a photo of children on horses outside their one-room school (Figure 2–3) might record "going to school" as a similarity but "riding a horse to school" under "Pioneer Children" and "taking a bus" under "Our Lives Today." After a reasonable amount of time, the groups exchange photos and begin new record sheets. If there are four groups, eventually each group will have examined four photos. The groups then share their record sheets for each photo with the class. Students are very interested in seeing how what they wrote compares with what other groups discovered. This exercise helps them begin to understand just how much you can find out by examining photographs. The next step is to repeat the exercise, but this time using diaries or memoirs.

Creating Time Lines and Maps

Many resources related to immigration or the movement west lend themselves to the creation of time lines and maps, which can be constructed in groups. Students must read the sources carefully in order to obtain the information they need to complete a time line or map. For example, a time line based on a child's diary of the journey west would include the date of each entry, a description and an illustration of what happened, and the location of the event. Each small group could create a different part of one time line, then all the parts could be pieced together and displayed.

Students can construct maps based on sources created by people who came to America from other countries, using yarn to trace their journeys and recording distances and lengths of time. Gluing quotes from journals and other sources onto a map personalizes the journey of each person whose immigration the map depicts.

Creating time lines and maps helps students develop a sense of time and place and to understand cause and effect. For example, a child's diary might begin with entries that sound as if the child is on an adventure, but as time and difficulties accumulate the entires might contain more and more negative comments. The time line or map for such a diary might show an incredibly long trip with rough terrain to cross, thus giving students a concrete illustration of why the entries became increasingly negative. Engaging students in these activities addresses the NCSS standards of demonstrating the ability to "construct simple timelines; identify examples of change; and recognize examples of cause and effect relationships" (1994, 34) and to create and use maps.

Using Resources to Motivate Participatory Citizenship

The experiences of children in history, whether they were Native Americans, pioneers, immigrants, in families of migrant workers, or lived during the Great Depression, remind us of the needs of people today. Students can draw connections between the historical accounts and the plight of modern-day homeless people, refugees, hungry people, people who need to feel welcomed and accepted, and people who lack friends.

This chapter has introduced a number of children who would be fine role models for today's students. These children fulfilled their responsibilities to their families and their wagon trains. They nursed the sick, guarded the wagons, and took care of young children. They reached out to others in need, and to those who were newly arrived from other countries. Birgitta Fichter, who emigrated from Sweden in 1924 at the age of six, recalled in an Ellis Island oral history interview:

> I turned seven after we got here and they put me in the first grade. I didn't know the language and every time the teacher even looked at me I would start to cry, because I was afraid. . . . But there was one little girl that I'll never forget. When it was recess time, this one girl came and put her arm around my shoulder. . . . took me outside, stayed with me during recess, and when recess was over she brought me back to my seat in school. (Etkin and Willoughby 1992, 43)

It is not hard to find modern children who have reached out to others. Many of us have heard of Trevor Ferrell's campaign to help the homeless. It began with eleven-year-old Trevor handing one blanket to one homeless man and went on to provide a thirty-three room boarding house for people who were homeless. Students can read about Trevor in the December 1993 issue of *Cobblestone* and in the book *Trevor's Place: The Story of the Boy Who Brings Hope to the Homeless* (Ferrell, Ferrell, and Wakin 1990).

Phillip Hoose's *It's Our World, Too!* describes how Dwaina Brooks' concern for the homeless and hungry began when her fourth-grade class did a unit on homelessness. Dwaina, her family, and her friends made food every Friday night to take to a shelter. By the time she was in sixth grade, Dwaina had organized several thousand meals. Her words and example can inspire our students to do something to help. "Kids should get going . . . We should try to help. . . . Each of us should have some kind of concern in our hearts for other people. And we owe it, too: there isn't a one of us who hasn't been helped by someone" (Hoose 1993, 60).

Paul Raccuglia's story is in *Kid Stories*, by Jim Delisle (1991). Paul tells how he helped a new boy from Afghanistan in his fourth-grade class: "He did speak English in a different kind of way. I helped him with his papers and some of the things he didn't know. I played with him at recess a lot. We got to be friends. . . . I learned that people from different countries can be a lot like you" (18–19). Delisle concludes Paul's story by asking readers to be aware of any students who have a hard time fitting in and to be a friend to them. He also suggests that students talk with their teachers and principals about making special arrangements to help new students adjust. When our students become friends with people who may seem different from them at first, they will find, as Paul did, that these new people are a lot like them after all.

Many children who help others are right in our own schools and communities. Arranging for our students to interview such children or inviting them to come to class and share what they are doing can motivate our students to take action and give them ideas about how to become involved. Community service agencies and organizations like the Boys and Girls Clubs, Campfire Girls, 4-H, Boy Scouts, and Girl Scouts might provide the names of young people your class could talk with. You can monitor the local newspaper for stories about children and young people helping others.

Your students will have ideas for things to do, such as donating food to food banks, donating needed items to shelters, raising money to give to organizations that help those in need, and even buying a goat or pig for Heifer International to give a struggling family in another country a way to earn money.

Here are some organizations to contact for other opportunities and information about how students can help others:

Habitat for Humanity International works to eliminate homelessness and poor housing. *www.habitat.org*

Heifer Project International gives animals to children and their families so they can earn money and produce their own food. *www.heifer.org*

The National Coalition for the Homeless works to end homelessness. *www.nationalhomeless.org*

The United Nations Children's Fund (UNICEF) helps children in developing countries who are living in poverty. *www.unicef.org*

The United Nations High Commission for Refugees provides help to people worldwide who have been forced to flee their homes. Free lesson plans, teaching materials, posters, and information about refugee children can be obtained through this agency. *www.unrefugees.org*

During the Great Depression, the hundreds of children who wrote letters to Eleanor Roosevelt took action to make their concerns known. Young people who moved from Oklahoma to California during the dust bowl days helped build a school at Weedpatch Camp. At the beginning of his journey west, eleven-year-old Elisha Brooks feared all Native Americans, but later in his journey, after trading with Sioux and getting to know members of the Crow tribe, his fear turned to admiration (West 1989, 36). As today's students become involved in helping others and in getting to know people who may at first seem different from them, they will find that they have much in common with young people past and present who have made a difference in others' lives.

3

Children Living During War, Children Working for Peace

When the families fled from Salem in 1777, Father had only a span of horses to aid in our flight. Mother and the youngest child rode one of these. Some of our goods and Samuel—who was sick at the time and but a small boy—was taken on the other. . . . We went down to Sancoick. . . . Word was brought us that the British army was coming that way. About a dozen Salem families were there. Everything was packed up in haste and we were ready to start the next morning, the army being encamped this night at Cambridge. . . . I went out in the morning to salt the sheep [provide salt for the animals. . . .]. Running to the top of the knoll and looking towards the house I saw . . . the soldiers . . . all about the house and neighborhood like a swarm of bees. I had but one thought—to run and join Father. . . . I got into the house in safety. The soldiers were plundering it of whatever they could find. One of them told Father to open the oven door, in which was an ovenful of bread just baked. Father did so, but one of the officers said, "Will you take the bread away from these children?" So they let it remain.

SIMON NELSON OF SALEM
(Adler 1998, 67–68)

When I read Jeanne Adler's *In the Path of War: Children of the American Revolution Tell Their Stories* (1998), I was reminded of the importance of viewing history from different perspectives and not just as a listing of events and facts. I had just read the above account of a young boy from Salem; a few pages later I came across the following:

While we were at Fort Edward, the Whigs tore down our fences and let the cattle into our grain fields, whereby it was nearly destroyed. Father had two horses which he took to Fort Edward. . . . "Mad" [James] More came with some men from Shushan, to drive off our cows. They threw down the fence and went to driving them out of the field, when Father got around them and drove them back. More then came up to him, and putting the muzzle of his loaded gun to Father's breast said, "Stand still, you . . . Tory or I'll shoot you through!" And the other men then drove the cattle away, while More kept Father away from them. They took them to Shushan and cast lots for them. One of them fell to Bill Smith, who the next day, drove her back home to us saying he could not take the milk from motherless children.

Caty Campbell of Greenwich (86–87)

I was amazed. Here were two accounts from the American Revolution that were strikingly similar even though the children were on opposite sides. Both expressed the terror that comes with war. One child's family feared the Tory militia; the other's feared the Whig militia. In both cases, soldiers raided the family's farm to get supplies—but at least one soldier showed concern for the children. Accounts of young people during wartime help illustrate the impact that war has on peoples' lives. Comparing such accounts can be an enlightening experience for today's students.

Teachers know that history is not just about events and facts; it also involves perspective. When we teach the American Revolution, the Civil War, or World War II, a major challenge is helping our students understand these events from the perspectives of the people involved. The National Council for the Social Studies (NCSS) standards emphasize including real people's experiences in instruction so that the students can "compare and contrast different stories or accounts about past events, people, places, or situations, identifying how they contribute to our understanding of the past" (NCSS 1994, 51). Helping students discover the perspectives of children who were caught up in war gives them a meaningful learning experience.

The American Revolution

There are a number of primary sources by or about children that teachers can use to give our students different perspectives on the American Revolution. The account of Sally (Sarah) Wister, a girl from a prominent Quaker family in Philadelphia, makes an interesting contrast to those of Simon Nelson and Caty Campbell, who lived on farms. When British troops were about to capture Philadelphia, Sally fled with her family to North Wales, Pennsylvania, to live with her aunt. She kept a diary, written as a letter to her cousin, that helps us understand what life was like for a wealthy Quaker family when Continental army officers stayed in their home.

Your students may be surprised to learn that young people near their age served as soldiers. Joseph Plumb Martin enlisted in the Continental army in 1776, when he was fifteen. His diary describes his experiences and hardships in camp, in battle, and marching.

> The British took possession of a hill overlooking us.... During the night we remained in our trenches.... The water was nearly over my shoes by morning. Many of us took violent colds.... I had nothing to eat or drink, not even water. In the evening a messmate found me & brought me boiled hog's flesh and turnips. (Martin 2001, 30)

Selections from the journals of John Greenwood and Ebenezer Fox provide students with the experiences of other boys in the war. John was thirteen when he began playing the fife for his uncle's company of militia (Coggins 1967) and fifteen when he enlisted as fifer in the Twelfth Massachusetts Bay Regiment, commanded by Colonel John Patterson. Ebenezer joined the Continental navy in Providence, Rhode Island, and served on the warship *Protector*. These boys' firsthand accounts provide students with fascinating reading of their views on different aspects of the war—including major battles, naval engagements, winters in General Washington's campaigns, hunger, illness, and even the surrender at Yorktown.

Young people who acted with courage demonstrated that they valued the American struggle. In Philadelphia, fourteen-year-old James Forten, of African ancestry, joined the crew of a privateer, which was one of the many private ships the American government allowed to capture British ships. His job was to bring gunpowder to the cannons on deck during battles. On his first voyage, his ship captured a British ship. On his second voyage it was captured. Although a prisoner, James became friends with the British captain's son. The captain offered to take James to England and pay for his education if he would renounce his allegiance to America. Refusing might mean that James would be sold as a slave in the West Indies or sent to prison. When the captain saw his hesitation he told him he certainly wouldn't be so foolish as to turn down his offer. James replied, "I'm afraid I must, Sir. I am here as a prisoner for the liberties of my country. I cannot prove a traitor to her interest" (Douty 1968, 44). Students can read about Forten in Esther Douty's *Forten the Sailmaker* or in *We Were There, Too!* by Phillip Hoose.

An important role for boys in the Revolutionary War was drummer for a military unit, some of whom were as young as nine. The drummers and fifers set the cadence for marching, signaled changes in strategy, and summoned the troops to battle. William Diamond signaled the troops with his drum when the British army was heading to Lexington and the American Revolution began (Collett 1989). He and other drummers served throughout the war.

Some girls were involved in the fighting, too. Deborah Sampson disguised herself as a boy called Robert Shirtliffe and fought in a regiment of the Continental army (Hoose 2001). Elizabeth Zane saved the colonists in Fort Henry by racing out of the fort—braving arrows and bullets—to fetch gunpowder from a nearby house (Etkin and Willoughby 1992). Many students know about the midnight ride of Paul Revere, but they may not know about a sixteen-year-old girl who also rode courageously. Her name was Sybil Ludington, and she rode thirty miles in the rain during the night to tell Colonel Ludington's soldiers to meet the British. Later General George Washington visited Sybil to personally thank her for her bravery (Amstel 2000).

Students will find accounts of children and young people braving danger while serving as spies to be exciting reading. In *We Were There, Too! Young People in U.S. History* (2001), Phillip Hoose describes the adventures of Mary Redmond, John Darragh, and Dicey Langston, who discovered British secrets and delivered them to the patriots.

In the years leading up to the Revolutionary War, many girls became active in patriotic sewing circles to protest British taxes. They met to spin and weave their own cloth, rather than import cloth from England. The girls had fun racing each other to spin the most yarn. They also used local herbs to make "liberty tea" instead of drinking British imports. One twelve-year-old girl, Anna Green Winslow, staying in Boston with her aunt, wrote to her father who happened to be a British military officer. "As I am (as we say) a daughter of liberty I chuse to wear as much of my own manufactory as pocible" (Carle, 1984, 32 in Hoose 2001, 49). Students wishing to find out more about Anna's life can read her diary, which is one of the few children's diaries surviving from this period (Earle 1974).

The Civil War

Resources by and about children in the Civil War era are also readily available. Girls and boys served in battle and at home. The role of the drummer boy continued to be important. Boys too young to be accepted as soldiers joined the army as drummer boys. They sometimes were involved in actual fighting or other duties if they were needed. One drummer boy described how he stayed at his position during battle in order to signal orders to the troops:

> A cannon ball came bouncing across the corn field kicking up dirt and dust each time it struck the earth. Many of the men in our company took shelter behind a stone wall, but I stood where I was and never stopped drumming. An officer came by on horseback and chastised the men, saying, "This boy puts you all to shame. Get up and move forward." We all began moving across the cornfield. . . . Even when the fighting was at its fiercest and I was frightened, I stood straight and did as I was ordered . . . I felt I had to be a good example for the others. (Murphy 1990, 43)

William Bircher wrote in his diary:

47

> January 1, 1863 Vandyke and I were the only ones left out of the eleven drummers
> . . . and . . . we had to do the entire guard duty. . . . November 15, 1864 . . . Marched
> nine miles to Atlanta, and at night we destroyed the city by fire. . . . (Bircher 2000,
> 15, 25)

Charles Miles Moore was a courageous member of the famous Fifty-Fourth Massachusetts black regiment. He and other young drummers helped soldiers move out
of the line of fire as they became wounded. Willie Johnston was under twelve
when he joined the third Vermont Infantry. When President Lincoln appeared for
the Vermont brigade's grand review after seven days of battle in 1862, Willie was
the only drummer who had been able to hold on to his drum throughout the battles; he played for Lincoln. In 1863, Willie was presented with the Medal of
Honor, the youngest soldier ever to receive this honor (Wisler 2001). These stories of courage stimulate student discussions about why and how young drummers
were involved in the war. What was so important to them about this war that they
would risk their lives?

Confederate and Union soldiers included boys sixteen and younger. Although
recruitment rules banned boys from fighting, they were able to slip in. In the
introduction to his book *The Boys' War* (1990), Jim Murphy gives an estimate
done by an army statistician after the war. Students are amazed to learn that 10 to
20 percent of soldiers were underage, which means that from 250,000 to 420,000
boys may have fought in the Civil War. Many sent letters home. Figure 3–1 shows
parts of letters that sixteen-year-old Private Charles Goddard wrote to his mother
from Camp Stone in 1861. Some young soldiers kept diaries or journals.

> Everything seemed to fascinate them . . . the long marches, the people they met along
> the way, the fighting, the practical jokes they played on one another. Even the mak-
> ing of bread was an event worth noting. . . . It is this directness and eye for everyday
> details that make the voices of these boys so fresh and believable and eloquent. And
> it is their ability to create active, vivid scenes that brings the war, in all its excitement
> and horror, alive after more than one hundred years. (Murphy 1990, 3)

The Jackdaw collection *Civil War: Young Soldiers* contains seventeen- by
twenty-two-inch photographs of boys involved in the war and a teacher's guide
for using them. Two of the preservice teachers in my social studies methods course
used this set in teaching fifth graders. When I came to observe, small groups of
students were scattered around the room, intently examining the photos. The
preservice teachers rotated the photos among the groups so that everyone had the
opportunity to study all twelve of them. The students seemed particularly fascinated by a photo of drummer boys in camp (Figure 3–2), and most groups noted
every detail of the scene. After the students had examined all the photographs,

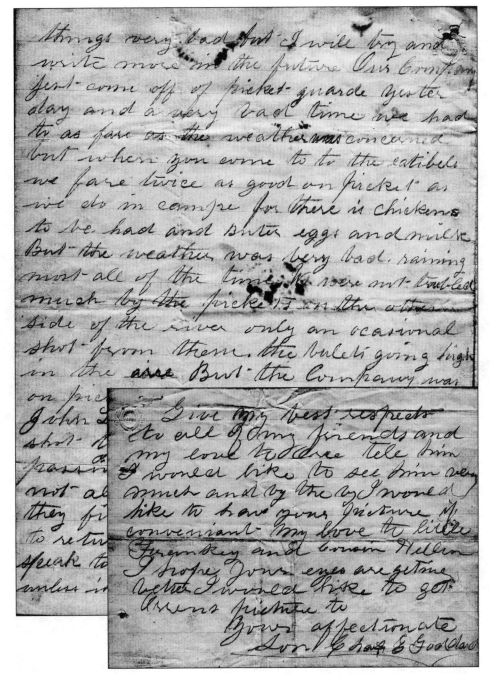

Figure 3–1. Excerpts from letters written in 1861 by Private Charles Goddard, age sixteen (courtesy of Minnesota Historical Society).

the preservice teachers engaged them in a discussion about what they had learned and what they thought it would be like to be one of the young soldiers pictured.

Diaries and letters written by both girls and boys reveal how the war affected those who remained at home. Alonzo Jefferies, a sixteen-year-old boy in Pennsylvania, kept a diary. In addition to daily occurrences, he wrote about news of the day and described troops arriving in his town:

> July 4th, 1863— . . . At 10 P.M. fifteen hundred paroled men (Union) arrived lately from the battle-field at Chamberburg. Alger and I were in bed, when we heard the deep-toned whistle of a locomotive of the Penna. Central Rail Road. . . . In a few moments we heard a great tramping of feet, and we bolted on our clothes and rushed down stairs and were soon out. Dirty, ragged, savage looking men were pouring by the house. From side to side the street was filled with them. I realized for the first time what an invasion was like.
>
> *Jefferies Diary at the Chester County Historical Society*

Figure 3–2. Ninety-third New York Infantry Drum Corps (courtesy of the Library of Congress, LC-B8171–7514).

A Confederate Girl: The Diary of Carrie Berry, 1864, is a juvenile book containing excerpts from the diary Carrie wrote as battles raged around and in Atlanta. On August 3 she wrote, "This was my birthday. I was ten years old, But I did not have a cake times were too hard so I celebrated with ironing. I hope by my next birthday we will have peace in our land so that I can have a nice dinner" (Berry 2000, 8). On August 4 she recorded, "The shells have ben flying all day and we have stayed in the cellar" (8). On November 16 she described the burning of Atlanta: "Oh, what a night we had. They came burning the store house and about night it looked like the whole town was on fire. We all set up all night. If we had not set up our house would have ben burnt up for the fire was very near and the soldiers were going around setting houses on fire where they were not watched" (23). A photograph of Carrie is in Figure 3–3.

In *We Were There, Too! Young People in U.S. History* (2001), Phillip Hoose describes contributions of girls during the Civil War. Fourteen-year-old Susie King Taylor was one of many African Americans in the South who escaped to the Union camps. Susie had learned to read and write, so a Union officer asked her to teach children and adults in the camp on St. Simons Island, Georgia. She began by teaching about forty children and a number of adults to read. Sixteen-year-old Emma Sansom helped her mother and sister run the family farm when her brothers joined the Confederate army. When the Union army blew up a bridge near her farm to keep the Confederate army from crossing, Emma guided Confederate General Nathan Forrest's troops to a place that was shallow enough to cross so that they could intercept the Yankee forces. The Confederate Congress gave Emma a gold medal for her help.

Two excellent adult books have excerpts by or about children in the Civil War era. In *Reluctant Witnesses: Children's Voices from the Civil War*, Emmy Werner uses the eyewitness accounts of 120 children, ages four to sixteen, to tell their stories, including the eyewitness accounts of emancipated slave children who joined the Union forces as "contraband soldiers" or enrolled in schools. Her primary sources are letters, journals, diaries, and the reminiscences of boys and girls from the Confederacy and the Union, both soldiers and civilians. The book also includes family members' and adult soldiers' impressions of children's experiences. Teachers can use this book to get a thorough overview of children's involvement in the Civil War, and can use sections of the book with their students. In the following interview, an African American woman recalls her childhood during the war years:

> I was a young gal, about ten years old, and . . . we hear that Lincoln gonna turn us free. Ol' Missus say there wasn't nothin to it. Then a Yankee soldier told someone . . . that Lincoln done signed the 'Mancipation. Was wintertime and mighty cold

Figure 3–3. Ten-year-old Carrie Berry, who lived in Atlanta, kept a diary in 1864 (Atlanta History Center).

that night, but everybody commenced getting ready to leave. Didn't care nothin 'bout Missus—was going to the Union lines. (Werner 1998, 39)

When your students read accounts of these and other children, they may be astounded at the responsibilities they assumed. For example, when Atlanta was under siege, ten-year-old Carrie Berry took care of her pregnant mother and sick younger sister. When the baby arrived, she cared for it and also cooked, cleaned, and sewed clothing for the family. After Atlanta was burned, Carrie and other children searched through the ruins looking for nails and lead to trade for food. Werner writes, "Yet she never lost a child's enthusiasm and joy of life! She was grateful for a lull in the shelling, for the large cellar in which she could romp about and her family could secretly hide, and for a little Christmas tree that she could decorate in the ruins of her burned-out city" (154).

Northern children took on adult responsibilities, too. Maria Lewis from Ebensburg, Pennsylvania, helped take care of younger siblings and the family farm when her father left to fight for the Union. At Gettysburg, young people went out during battle to help injured soldiers. "I never thought I could do anything about a wounded man," wrote Jeannie McCreary after the battle was over, "but find that I had a little bit more nerve than I thought I had" (154).

Here are the voices of children on opposing sides of the war. Their experiences can stimulate classroom discussion about how young people on both sides faced hardships and new responsibilities. They might also lead your students to talk about times that they were able to do things that they had thought they couldn't do.

Modern-day students find it interesting to read about how teachers offered emotional support and how books became a refuge for children who stayed at home. Many girls wrote about favorite teachers who encouraged them to continue with schoolwork in spite of the war. Werner describes how Celine Fremaux of Baton Rouge walked to school hearing gunfire from riverboats and seeing decaying bodies. Children sat for days in dark cellars, listening to bombs and shells, often reading to pass the time. Emma LeConte wrote in her diary:

> If it had not been for my books [the war] would, indeed, have been hard to bear. But in them I have lived and found my chief source of pleasure. I would take refuge in them from the sadness all around. (155)

The Children's Civil War, by James Marten, is another valuable resource for teachers. Marten describes how the war affected children's literature, schoolbooks, and schools. One New Orleans school used recess time to produce lint to pack into wounds. This process was called *scraping* or *picking.*

When nine year old Maurice Egan and his Philadelphia friends failed to get into the army as drummers, he complained that they "were reduced to making lint for the army" with girls. (Marten 1998, 177)

Marten quotes Clara Lenroot's reflections about her role in the Soldier's Aid Society meetings at her church:

Very important we children felt . . . as we scraped away at the linen making fluffy piles of the soft lint "for the soldiers." (177)

They comforted each other and read aloud letters from loved ones describing battles, camps, and even prison escapes.

World War II

Students studying World War II can create their own primary sources by interviewing senior citizens who were young during the war. Recording interviews and sharing them with their classmates give children an excellent inquiry experience. Chapter 2 includes some guidelines for preparing students to conduct interviews. They can ask questions like How did your life change during the war? How did you contribute to the war effort? How did the war affect your school experiences? Some students might be lucky enough to interview a person who kept a diary or received letters from a soldier.

The Diary of Anne Frank is perhaps the best-known primary source created by a young person during World War II, but a number of other juvenile books include memoirs of wartime childhoods. *The Hidden Children*, by Howard Greenfeld, is the result of his interviews with thirteen Jewish men and women who as children went into hiding to survive the Holocaust. Unlike Anne Frank, who was among the 1.5 million young Jews who died (Greenfeld), these thirteen lived to tell their stories. Zelda Polofsky described how her family hid with a farmer:

He had a house, like a barn, for hay. Before he put the hay in, he put in a structure, and we would climb through the hay on our knees, all the way to the structure, unable to see there. And that is when my mother died. . . . The man couldn't give us too much food. He didn't have enough for himself. (Greenfeld 1992, 82)

My mother, whatever food she had . . . maybe it would have kept her alive—she gave it to me. And I took it, never questioning. (81)

People from around the world and from every walk of life contributed their recollections of growing up during World War II to *Children of the Storm: Childhood Memories of World War II*, by Charles Perkins. The book contains many fascinating and moving photographs, including one of children in Butte, Montana, on top of a mountain of scrap metal that they collected to be recycled as planes, ships, and tanks; one of Russian schoolchildren studying at desks in the bombed ruins of their Leningrad school; and one of children wearing gas masks in a class-room in England. It is organized along broad-based themes such as rationing, school, food, and the home front. A group of students that chose one of the themes would find enough information in the book to create posters or displays on the theme. The book is especially interesting because people of many different nationalities shared their memories with Perkins. Erwin Perrot, born in Germany in 1934, recalled:

> Early in the war, we had prisoners of war as labor for our family's commercial truck farm. We had French and Russian prisoners who lived with my grandparents. They were all good people. We could see that they were people just like us. One of the Russians—Alex—used to take me riding on the bicycle. My grandparents would let us go everywhere together and no one worried about it. (Perkins 1998, 121)

Jean Holder recalled her experiences at a school in London when she was ten:

> When the air raids started, all the children felt a great deal of stress. We were taken to the downstairs cloakrooms, which had bricked-up windows, and older girls would read poetry and prose to us while the raid was going on. . . . Paper was very scarce. To save paper, we had to write on the covers of our exercise books, inside and out. In the wide margins at the top of the page we had to draw extra lines. At home, if you received an envelope, you sliced it open, reversed it, and made it into scrap paper. We also used to have a map of the war on the wall. . . . The children in the class used to take it in turns to move the pins indicating the front lines and the places that Allied troops had captured. Everyone liked being in charge of the Russian map because their front had started moving earlier and it was moving faster! (48)

In the December 1985 issue of *Cobblestone*, Priscilla Harding describes how as an eight-year-old she helped the war effort by collecting scrap metal and how her family coped with food rationing and the shortages of goods. In the January 1994 issue, Elizabeth Irvine recalls what it was like being an American teenage prisoner of war in the Philippines when the Japanese occupied Manila.

Echoes of World War II, by Trish Marx (1994), is based on interviews with six people who spent parts of their childhoods involved in World War II. One of the people was from a Jewish family in Germany. Another, who was born in Nor-mandy, France, lived in Hungary and Sweden during the war because her father was a diplomat. The others lived in England, Japan, Germany, and the Philippines. Students who read this book will get an in-depth view of these children's lives.

A study of World War II would not be complete without including the intern-ment of Japanese Americans following the attack on Pearl Harbor. Books such as

I Am an American, by Jerry Stanley (1994), and the Jackdaw collection of photographs of families in the camps can help students understand what these children and their families experienced. Canadian families of Japanese origin were also placed in internment camps for three years. Shizuye Takashima, who was a child in one of these prison camps, wrote and drew about what it was like in her book *A Child in Prison Camp* (1989).

The Children of Topaz: The Story of a Japanese-American Internment Camp (Tunnell and Chilcoat 1996) is based on a diary kept by a third-grade class in this camp in Utah (Figure 3–4). The teacher, Miss Yamauchi, recorded what the children wanted to put in their diary, and the children illustrated each of the seventy-three pages. The entries are fascinating because they reveal not only the injustices in the camp, but also the children's ability to find some joy in their new desert world. As I read this book, I marveled at the teacher's ability to create as normal a school life as possible for these children in spite of the harsh environment and unfair treatment. It is interesting to note that the children in this camp supported the war effort through collecting nails and working in a victory garden (Figure 3–5), just as many children on the outside did. Modern-day students reading diary

Figure 3–4. Pages from a diary kept by a third-grade class in an internment camp in 1943 (photographs of diary pages courtesy of Michael O. Tunnell; diary pages used by permission of the Utah State Historical Society). *Continued on next page.*

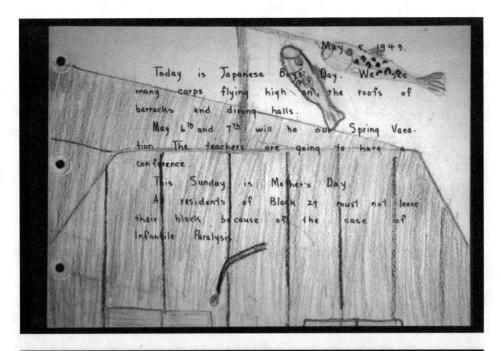

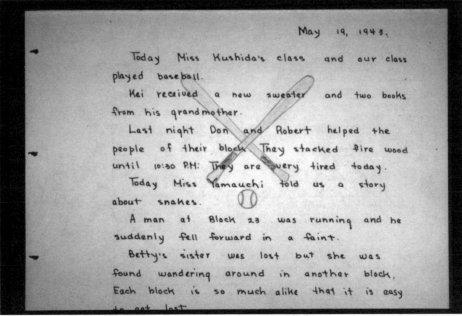

Figure 3–4. *Continued.*

entries like this one can look for sentences that reveal injustices and statements that reflect efforts to lead a normal life.

When President Roosevelt signed the order for the imprisonment of people of Japanese descent, seventh-grade teacher Ella Evanson received farewell letters from her students who had to go to the camps. She preserved those letters. Yoon Pak includes typed copies of some of the letters along with teaching suggestions in an article in *Middle Level Learning* (Pak 2001). Pak suggests having students discuss what the letters reveal about these young people's thoughts and feelings about their teacher, school, and country.

Children Working for Peace

Through sharing their experiences living in war, children have increased other people's awareness of the need to work for peace. As these children served as drummer boys, collected scrap metal, joined patriotic sewing circles, and made other contributions they were working for peace in their own ways. They describe their lives immersed in war, but the children also express their desire for peace.

Figure 3–5. Children in the Topaz internment camp planting a victory garden (courtesy of the Utah State Historical Society).

At age eleven, Zlata Filipović of Sarajevo began writing in her diary about the war surrounding her (Figure 3–6).

> I keep wanting to explain these stupid politics to myself, because it seems to me that politics caused this war. . . . It looks to me as though these politics mean Serbs, Croats and Muslims. But they are all people. They are all the same. . . . But now there's "something" that wants to make them different. . . . Among my girl friends . . . there are Serbs and Croats and Muslims . . . but I never knew who was a Serb, a Croat or a Muslim. Now politics has started meddling around. . . . Why is politics making us unhappy, separating us . . . ? I simply don't understand it. Of course, I'm "young," and politics are conducted by "grown ups." But I think we "young" would do it better. We certainly wouldn't have chosen war. (Filipović 1994, 102–103)

In 1982, Samantha Smith, a ten-year-old American girl, was so concerned about world peace that she wrote to Yuri Andropov, the new leader of what was then the Soviet Union. He wanted her to see that the Soviet Union desired peace so he invited her to visit him. Samantha suggested that getting to know others better was a way to work for peace.

Figure 3–6. Zlata Filipović, at her home in Sarajevo, kept a diary as war surrounded her (Alexandra Boulat/SIPA Press).

It seemed strange to even talk about war when we all got along so well together. I guess that's what I came to find out. I mean, if we could be friends by just getting to know each other better, then what are our countries really arguing about? Nothing could be more important than not having a war. (Belcher-Hamilton 1989, 9)

Students may be interested in reading the book Samantha wrote, *Samantha Smith: Journey of the Soviet Union.*

Recently, a colleague gave me a copy of an article in the May 2, 2003, issue of the *Christian Science Monitor* that included the diary of a fourteen-year-old Iraqi girl, Amal Hussein, pictured in Figure 3–7. She writes about praying for peace, preparing for the invasion of Baghdad, her fears during the bombing, and the arrival of the American soldiers.

> Monday, March 17: . . . War is torment. . . . War takes away people we love. . . . We prepare by filling water buckets in case there is no water or electricity. Duha and Hibba pray God Almighty that there will be no war. At 8:30, my mother made bread. Bakeries close during the war.
>
> Friday, March 21: Today is Baghdad's turn. At 8:10 p.m., the siren was heard. [Friend] Omar was talking about war when a missile flew just over the building. Then at 9, the bombing was louder; [we] were crying . . . for God to bring the morning.

Figure 3–7. Amal Hussein, age fourteen, who lives in Bagdad, writes in her diary about the war as her mother and a sister watch (Scott Peterson/Getty Images).

Monday April 14: At 1:55 p.m., the twins come home and say Americans are walking on the street, and writing their names on children's hands. Hibba's hands have soldiers' names written on them. [The twins] say the soldiers were nice.... Are they really nice? Nobody knows but God. (8–9)

Our students can be inspired to work for peace through the examples of the children in this chapter. One class of third- and fourth-grade students in Albuquerque, New Mexico, was motivated by the actions of children in Hiroshima. They heard the story *Sadako and the Thousand Paper Cranes* (Coer 1977), which tells of Sadako's effort to fold a thousand paper cranes in an attempt to recover from the effects of the dropping of the bomb. When they found out that children in Hiroshima raised money to build a peace statue of Sadako there, they decided to build one in Los Alamos, New Mexico. Why there? Because the bomb dropped on Hiroshima had been built in Los Alamos. The children formed a Kids' Committee to Build a Peace Statue, held a press conference, and attracted supporters. The day after the press conference, an editorial supporting them appeared in the *Albuquerque Journal*. The editorial said:

These students, ages 5 to 17, are learning, organizing, planning, assuming responsibility, working toward a goal and making commitments. Keep it up, keep it growing and this world will more likely see further generations of peace. (Hoose 1993, 121)

Students can increase other students' awareness of the need to work for peace by telling them about young people like Zlata, Amal, Samantha, and the fourth-grade children in Albuquerque. For example, they might do this by creating a power point presentation on these or other inspiring young people to show to other classes. Following the presentation, they can ask for ideas about how to get involved and then share some of their own ideas. In addition, they could ask if anyone is already taking action and what they are doing.

Key questions that we teachers can ask our students to guide them in working for peace include:

What would young people living in a past time of war want us to do about conflict and wars today?
How many ways can we think of that we can work for peace?
Which one of these ways do we want to start working on now?

Students may choose to work on ways of handling conflict in their own classroom, school, home, and local community, or they may decide to do it on a more global basis. Students can start a fund for peace and raise money to donate to organizations working for peace. They can march for peace or write letters to the local newspaper giving their opinions. They can contact their senators and

61

representatives and encourage them to work for peace. Talking to people who are involved in peace issues can help students learn about approaches they can take. Hearing about what other students have done and are doing today will give them ideas.

Once students decide what they want to do to work for peace, whether it's participating in conflict management in their school, creating public awareness of peace issues, or some other activity, they need to determine what steps to take to accomplish their goals. If there is a person, a group, or an agency already involved in doing what the students want to do, a first step would be to make contact. If there isn't, they might begin by brainstorming about what strategies they could use or researching strategies that others have used successfully. Books like *The Kid's Guide to Social Action* by Barbara Lewis (1998) or *It's Our World, Too!* by Phillip Hoose (1993) are written for students and can provide guidance about ways of working for peace. Empowered by the examples of children in the past and children today, our students too can be successful in working for peace. In doing so, they demonstrate their ability to "practice forms of civic discussion and participation consistent with the ideals of citizens in a democratic society" (NCSS 1994, 44).

A Vietnamese woman, Phan Thi Kim Phue, wrote in her memoirs about being injured in an air attack when she was a child said, "I have suffered a lot. . . . But God saved my life and gave me faith and hope. . . . We cannot change history, but we should try to do good things for the present and the future" (Werner 1998, 159). As teachers, we all hope that our students will "do good things for the present and the future."

Using the Resources

There are a number of ways of incorporating these sources by or about real children into a study of any of these periods of war. Introducing a study by reading and discussing selections from diaries and showing photographs of the children motivates students to want to find out more about these historical children and what happened then. For example, after hearing the accounts of a Tory child and a Whig child quoted at the beginning of this chapter, students would have many questions about the Tories and the Whigs, such as why they were fighting and how the children were involved. The account in Jim Murphy's book *The Boys' War* (1990), describing a Civil War battle in which the drummer boy kept drumming while cannon balls bounced across the cornfield and the men hid would certainly be a motivating beginning to a lesson. It might also stimulate students' feelings of pride that someone near their age showed such incredible bravery.

Diary selections can be used as examples of effects of war. The girls who were active in patriotic sewing circles where they made their own cloth and used their own herbal teas illustrate the American protest of British taxes. The photographs of the Japanese American families in internment camps during World War II and the photographs and stories of those who hid to survive the Holocaust illustrate the suffering and mistreatment of innocent people.

Students can conduct an inquiry into any aspect of these wars. For example, when learning about what happened on the home front, they could research ways that children helped. Their results could be presented in creative ways, such as staging an awards ceremony and presenting certificates or medals. Students pretending to be children who collected the most scrap metal for World War II or elementary school children during the Civil War who produced the most lint for use in the hospitals would receive the awards. Students could create posters or flyers announcing the ceremony, including pictures of those to be honored and descriptions of what they did. For information about how to engage students in inquiry, refer to Chapter 2.

Analyzing Primary Sources

Teachers know that before we study any event, it is necessary to establish the historical context with our students. A meaningful way to do this is to guide your students in analyzing the writings and photographs of children who lived during the period you are studying. They can search for clues about what children's lives were like then. Students can work in pairs or individually to look at a variety of resources and list their findings, which can then be combined into a composite list for the class. You can then help connect the historical children with your students' ways of living today by creating a Venn diagram or another graphic comparing similarities and differences in their lives.

For example, in a study of the Civil War, students can analyze the diaries of the Confederate girl Carrie Berry and the Union drummer boy William Bircher, using the guide sheets in Figures 3–8 and 3–9. To examine photographs of young soldiers such as those in *The Boys' War* by Jim Murphy or in the Jackdaw Civil War photo collection and draw inferences from these photographs, students can use the guide in Figure 3–10.

Comparing Sources

A way of using these resources that encourages higher-level thinking is for students to compare their findings from analyzing primary sources with an analysis of secondary sources. For example, a composite class list about the way children lived

Guide to Analyzing the Writings
of Young Soldiers, Drummers, or Fifers

1. Read a diary, journal, memoir, or the letters of a soldier, drummer, or fifer.

2. Write your reaction to what you read. How did you feel as you read? What did you think?

3. Why do you think the writer wrote this?

4. On which side is this person serving? Where is he from? Find it on a map.

5. Read the writing a second time. Fill in this chart as you read.

Jobs and Responsibilities	Dangers	Hardships	Food, Clothing, and Shelter	Ways of Keeping Safe

6. What do you have in common with this person? In what ways are you like him? How are you different?

7. Choose one of the following activities:

    a. Create an illustrated time line showing what is happening in this person's life.

    b. Write letters responding to what he wrote, asking questions and telling about your life on the home front. You might pretend to be a brother, sister, cousin, or friend of the person.

Figure 3–8. Guide to Analyzing the Writings of Young Soldiers, Drummers, or Fifers.

Guide to Analyzing the Writings of Young People on the Home Front

1. Read a diary, journal, memoir, or the letters of a young person on the home front.

2. On a sheet of drawing paper, using different colors of markers or crayons, list words that describe your feelings and reactions to what the person wrote. Select colors that express your feelings as you write.

3. On which side of the war is this person? Where does he or she live? Find the place on a map.

4. Who is in the person's family? Who lives with him or her and who in the family is serving in the military?

5. Read the writing of this person a second time. As you read, fill in the chart below:

Responsibilities at Home	How Person Helped War Effort	Ways of Having Fun	Schoolwork	Food, Clothes, and Home	Hardships and Dangers, Ways of Keeping Safe, Feelings

6. What do you have in common with this young civilian? In what ways are you different?

7. Choose one of the following activities:

   a. Create an illustrated time line showing what is happening in this person's life.

   b. Write a letter to this person responding to what they wrote, telling what you are doing, and asking questions. You might pretend to be a soldier, another civilian, a family member, or a friend.

Figure 3–9. Guide to Analyzing the Writings of Young People on the Home Front.

Guide to Analyzing Photographs of Young Soldiers

1. Choose a photograph of young soldiers.

2. Look closely at the photograph for several minutes.

3. List all the words, phrases, and ideas that come to your mind as you look at it.

4. Look closely again at the photograph. On a large sheet of drawing paper, sketch an outline map of the photograph. Label each part that you sketched. Then write words describing the scene, soldiers, objects, and activities inside or near what you sketched.

5. Pretend that you can step into the photograph and talk to the soldiers.

    a. What are they saying to you?
    b. What questions do you ask them?
    c. What are they thinking, feeling, and wishing?
    d. How old do you think each soldier is?
    e. What sounds do you hear?
    f. What do you smell? Touch?
    g. How do you feel about being there with them?

6. What have you learned about the soldiers and their lives just by looking at the photograph?

7. List what you have in common with any of the soldiers. For example, if one of them is playing a drum or fife, maybe you have also played one of those instruments.

8. Choose one of the following activities to do:

    a. Write a caption for this photograph that shows what you have learned.

    b. Find a picture of modern-day soldiers. List what is alike between the two photographs, then list what is different.

Figure 3–10. Guide to Analyzing Photographs of Young Soldiers.

during the Civil War can be compared with the content of such children's books as *If You Lived at the Time of the Civil War* by Kay Moore (1994) or the American Kids in History series book *Civil War Days*. A list related to World War II can be compared with *World War II Days* by David King (2000). This comparison helps students understand the value of using primary sources, which lets them use the processes that real historians use, as well as the differences between the two kinds of resources.

A third kind of comparison is to look at primary sources in relation to each other. For example, the interviews students collect of people who grew up in World War II can be compared with interviews recorded by others, such as Priscilla Harding's description of collecting scrap metal and coping with food rationing when she was eight years old. The recollections of people who survived the Holocaust in *The Hidden Children* (Greenfield 1993) can be compared with primary sources created during the Holocaust, such as the diary of Anne Frank. The writings of children on the Union and Confederate sides of the Civil War or who were from Whig and Tory families during the American Revolution are fascinating to compare. Students can use guides like those in Figures 3–11 and 3–12 to make these kinds of comparisons.

These in-depth approaches to analyzing and comparing are based on a view of teaching that develops historical understanding. Spending more time on fewer topics during the school year is important because it lets students become immersed in a subject or time period. "Proponents of this view contend that in-depth approaches give students better opportunities to construct knowledge in ways that form lasting historical schemas that connect to their everyday lives" (Brophy and VanSledright 1997, 28).

Creating from Different Perspectives

Perhaps one of the most valuable uses of these sources is to engage students in activities that help them understand the variety of perspectives of the children living in the time period they're studying. Each student in a class can take on the role of a real child living during the war that's being studied and be interviewed by the class. The student studies the writings and photograph of the real child so as to pretend to be that child. On the day of the interviews, each student dresses as a real child, tells that child's story, and answers questions. The different roles and perspectives can then be recorded on a chart. For example, if you are studying the Civil War, students can be drummer boys, Union soldiers, Confederate soldiers, spies, or children living at home in the South and in the North.

Some students, like fourteen-year-old Justin Harris, pursue perspective-taking outside the classroom. Justin joined the Ninth Texas Infantry reenactors as a

Guide for Comparing Young Soldiers' Writings on Opposite Sides of the War

1. Read the writings of a soldier on each side of the war.

2. Complete the chart in the "Guide to Analyzing the Writings of Young Soldiers, Drummers, or Fifers" for each writing you read.

3. Record the information from each guide on the chart below:

	Soldier X	Soldier Y
Jobs and Responsibilities		
Hardships		
Dangers		
Food, Clothing, and Shelter		
Location		
Feelings		
Ways of Keeping Safe		

4. Look at the information you recorded on the chart. What do these two people have in common? What is different? Do they have more things in common than differences? Why or why not?

Figure 3–11. Guide for Comparing Young Soldiers' Writings on Opposite Sides of the War.

Guide for Comparing Young Soldiers' Writings with Writings of Young People on the Home Front

1. Read the writings of a soldier, drummer, or fifer.

2. Complete the chart in the "Guide to Analyzing the Writings of Young Soldiers, Drummers, or Fifers."

3. Read the writings of a person on the home front.

4. Complete the chart in the "Guide to Analyzing the Writings of Young People on the Home Front."

5. Record the information from each guide on the chart below:

	Military Person	Home Front Person
Jobs and Responsibilities		
Hardships		
Dangers		
Food, Clothing, and Shelter		
Location		
Ways of Keeping Safe		
Feelings		

6. Look at the information you recorded. What do these two people have in common? What is different? Do they have more things in common than differences? Why or why not?

Figure 3–12. Guide for Comparing Young Soldiers' Writings with the Writings of Young People on the Home Front.

drummer and has experienced some of what the young drummers in the Civil War did. He wants to be as historically accurate as possible in his portrayal. He and the other young people in his infantry believe it is important for people to remember the contributions made by the Civil War drummers. Wisler (2001), who wrote about Justin in his book on young people in the Civil War, states, "So long as young people remain interested in the stories of the youngest soldiers of the Civil War and living historians such as Justin portray their lives, they will not be forgotten" (98).

Another way to help students understand events from the point of view of historical children is for them to pretend to be living back then and create journals, diaries, or letters similar to the primary sources they are reading. In order to do this, students have to really immerse themselves in the time period through research. Students enjoy perspective-taking activities. Levstik and Barton (1997) describe the experiences of two teachers who used perspective-taking assignments. The students wrote poems, journals, letters, and editorials and did other activities from the perspective of the historical people. "In both classrooms students consistently pointed to these kinds of perspective-taking activities as one of the primary reasons they enjoyed studying history" (131). Some students reported not liking history until they started pretending to be the historical people they were studying.

Students can make history come alive when they engage in drama. Creating scenes from Carrie Berry's Civil War diary, *The Boys' War*, James Forten's experience on a privateer during the Revolutionary War, *Children of the Storm*, or any of the other resources described here, makes these children's lives in the wars seem real. Acting can be spontaneous, with just a few props, or the students can develop a play with costumes and scenery.

Using Simulations

Simulations offer the opportunity for students to put themselves in the roles of these children, face the problems they faced, and make decisions about what they would do if they were actually there. When I am planning a simulation, I look through the resources to find situations with problem-solving opportunities that would be appropriate to use. For example, in a study of World War II a simulation could involve deciding whether or not to hide Jewish children in your home.

For a simulation to be effective, the students should not know what decisions the actual person made until the simulation is over. The teacher sets the scene and the problem. For the American Revolutionary period, James Forten's experiences described in Hoose (2001) could be worked into a simulation. Forten is faced with the decision of whether to stay and help his family, who lived in poverty since his father had died, or to be a privateer. He knows that his family needs his help, but he also knows that a privateer's wages are good. He is aware of the risks involved in being a privateer, including the possibility of being captured by the British. Students can weigh all of these facts and decide what they would do. When James does become a privateer and is captured, he must decide whether to renounce his allegiance to America and accept the British captain's offer of a paid education in England, or risk the alternatives of either being shipped to the West Indies to be a slave or going to a British prison ship. What would your students do if they were James? Why? What do they need to consider in order to decide?

Asking questions like the following will help direct students' thinking as they engage in simulations:

What would you do? Why?
What are your choices? Are there any other possible alternatives?
What are the advantages, disadvantages, and consequences of each choice?

After the simulation, help students make connections to their own lives by asking them to tell about similar situations they have faced, such as standing up for what they believe is right even though it means not being popular with their peers. Participating in simulations where they face situations that real people near their own age faced in the past makes history come alive for students and helps them make connections with their lives today.

Making Connections Today

Another way of making connections with students' lives today is to help them become acquainted with modern-day children who recently experienced or currently are experiencing wars. Students can look for newspaper and magazine articles on areas where wars, conflicts, and violence are occurring now. They can clip out pictures and articles to place in a class scrapbook or on a bulletin board or poster. Unfortunately, such articles are not hard to find. After writing this paragraph I looked at the first page of the *New York Times* on my kitchen table. I saw a picture of a young boy and his father who were victims of riots in India. The next day there was an article about a fourteen-year-old Palestinian girl killed in fighting between Jewish settlers and Palestinians.

Children in the latter part of the twentieth century and the first part of the twenty-first have written about their experiences living in war-torn areas. Your students can compare these writings with the experiences of the young people in history they are studying. They might also be motivated to keep journals of their feelings and thoughts about the wars and conflicts in different parts of the world today.

Perhaps the best known war diary written by a modern-day young person is the one by Zlata Filipović. She wrote her diary in Sarajevo, Bosnia, from about age eleven through age thirteen. Students may find it interesting to hear that Zlata was influenced by another girl in history: Before war came to Sarajevo, Zlata had read Anne Frank's diary. Like Anne Frank, Zlata wrote to an imaginary friend. Zlata said in an interview, "In a way we were in the same position . . . writing a diary, lonely, can't go outside, losing our childhood. The difference is she was in an attic and I was in a cellar" (Riding 1994, 16). I wonder if Amal Hussein had read either Anne's or Zlata's diary and might have been motivated by one of them to write her own diary during the war in Iraq?

As part of a closure to a study of any war, students can examine the writings and stories of the children living then, focusing on questions such as the following:

- What did the children who survived the war have in common?
- What can we learn from them?
- What is going on in my life that is somewhat similar to what they experienced?
- What helped them get through those difficult times?
- What helps us get through difficult times today?

As your students discuss these questions, they may find that they have a lot in common with these children. They also may come to value the contributions of both historical and contemporary young people, and find inspiration for their own lives. Emmy Werner says,

> They were children who loved life. They were not bitter; they did not hate. The wars that shaped their lives were fought in the name of causes that adults believed in and were willing to kill for . . . [They] survived, hoping, against all odds, that some day there might be the possibility of peace. (1998, 159)

Carrie Berry showed this desire for peace when she wrote in her diary, "I hope that by my next birthday we will have peace in our land so that I can have a nice dinner" (Berry 2000, 8).

4

Children in Slavery, Children Laboring and Striking

I started when I was twelve years old. My mother brought me to the mill. . . . We went to work at 6 o'clock and stopped at 6. . . . We didn't get out doors when we had our lunch, we eat in the baggin' room. I was spinning. . . . I feel tired . . . ; I go barefoot in the mill, it's too hot to wear shoes. . . . The lint flies so you have to chew so you can swallow.

BERTIE MAY BERRY
Testimony of a child worker in the Fulton Bag and Cotton Mills, taken at the Strike Headquarters, July 28th, 1914. (National Archives, RG 174 in West 1996, 35–36)

I worked in a lower room where I had heard the proposed strike fully, if not vehemently, discussed; . . . When the day came on which the girls were to turn out, those in the upper rooms started first. . . . Then, when the girls in my room stood irresolute, uncertain what to do . . . I, who began to think they would not go out, after all their talk, became impatient, and started on ahead, saying, . . . "I don't care what you do, I am going to turn out . . . ;" and I marched out and was followed by the others. As I looked back at the long line that followed me, I was more proud than I have ever been.

HARRIET HANSON [ROBINSON], *who at age eleven helped to lead a strike in 1836 at a Lowell mill. (Robinson 1976, 52)*

We arrived at Baltimore. . . . I was conducted to Mr. and Mrs. Auld. . . . And I was told to take care of little Thomas. . . . My new mistress. . . . had never had a slave under her control previously to myself. . . . She very kindly commenced to teach me the A, B, C. After I had learned this, she assisted me in learning to spell words of three or four letters. Just at this point of my progress, Mr. Auld found out what was going on, and at once forbade Mrs. Auld to instruct me further, telling her, among other things, that it was unlawful, as well as unsafe, to teach a slave to read. . . . From that moment, I understood the pathway from slavery to freedom. . . . Though conscious of the difficulty of learning without a teacher, I set out . . . to learn how to read.

FREDERICK DOUGLASS, *who at eight was sent to the Aulds in 1825.*
(Douglass 1994, 11–13)

I am an eleven-year-old boy working in the brick kilns for the past six years. . . . We go to work around 2 A.M. . . . and return by 6 P.M. . . . I am given no time to play. . . . My hope is to enjoy freedom, if I am released from bondage.

ASHIG, *a bonded slave in Pakistan about 1997.*
(Whittaker 1998, 19 in Kuklin 1998, 29–30)

I am seated on the floor surrounded by Lewis Hine's photographs of child laborers taken at the beginning of the twentieth century and photographs of children who were slaves on plantations in the South prior to the end of the Civil War. The expressions on these children's faces and the visible evidence of their desperate situations trouble me. I remember observing a lesson by one of my education students in a fifth-grade classroom. The class had just finished examining photographs from the Jackdaw photograph collection *Child Labor, the Shame of the Nation* and had many questions and concerns. A major concern was that children could be treated this way. "Didn't people care what happened to them back then?" one student asked. "That couldn't happen today," another said in a confident voice, unaware that, in fact, there are both slavery and child labor in our world today. At first glance, modern-day students might think that all the quotes opening this chapter are from children in the past. But, the last one is not history—it's current! Ashig lives in Pakistan and may have been freed since his interview with a human rights monitor. He is representative of the many children still toiling or in bondage throughout the world. In this chapter, I introduce children who were slaves and children who were child laborers in the Industrial Revolution through the early part of the twentieth century, as well as some contemporary children in similar situations.

Children in Slavery

In America, children living in slavery were forced into hard work from a very young age. Harriet Tubman was only three when she began picking cotton

74

(Hoose 2001). Most children who were slaves were treated cruelly and not allowed to learn to read or write. Tonya Bolden, in *Tell All the Children Our Story* (2001), and Sylviane Diouf, in *Growing Up in Slavery* (2001), describe the lives of children who were captured and sold as slaves and children who were born into slave families. These books are two of the best I have found to give students information about the lives and work of children who were slaves. They provide good introductions before going more in-depth with the stories of specific children.

Our students may be able to give an adequate definition of the word *slave*. They may even be able to describe in general how slaves were treated and what they did. However, they may not know what it was actually like to live as a slave or be able to view life from a slave's perspective. Reading or hearing accounts of people who were captured and sold into slavery as children or who were born as slaves provides an authentic experience that enables students to "develop new understanding through a process of active construction of knowledge" (NCSS 1994, 12). When they come to know the stories of slaves who were near their own ages, the word *slave* takes on new meaning. Examining photographs of children in slavery helps the historical children become real to our students. The photographs in this chapter and the excerpts of recollections of former slaves are but a few of the sources available for teachers to use with our students.

Two of the preservice teachers in my social studies methods course used these resources in teaching fifth-grade students about children in slavery as part of their unit on the Civil War. The cooperating teacher and I observed as they read selections from *Escape from Slavery: The Boyhood of Frederick Douglass in His Own Words* (Douglass 1994). After some discussion, the preservice teachers told the students that each group would receive an excerpt of a childhood recollection of a former slave, along with a related photograph or sketch. The two preservice teachers explained to the children how to use a question sheet to help them examine these sources, then handed out the materials. A recorder was to write each group's answers on the question sheet. One group received an account of living conditions and a photograph of children in front of slave cabins. Another was given a former slave's description of working and a photograph of child and adult slaves in a cotton field (Figure 4–1). A third group received an excerpt about efforts to learn to read and a photograph that shows a child reading a Bible (Figure 4–2). Another group was given an account of what children who were slaves did in their rare free time and photos of children dancing in front of a slave cabin (Figure 4–3), of a rag doll, and of clay marbles. The last group got narratives and pictures about slave auctions and food.

As the groups began studying their resources, I wandered around the room observing their reactions and listening to their comments. One group was

Figure 4–1. Children in slavery working in a cotton field (collection of the New York Historical Society).

responding to a question about how they felt about the ways the slaves had to live and were treated. Here is what I heard:

It is cruel.
I feel sad.
I feel mad.
I wish I could go back in time and help them out.
I feel bad because I am free and all I have to do is dishes and keep my room clean.
If I was there I would stop that madness.

Another group was responding to a question about what they would ask the children or say to them if they could step into the photograph. Some of them were expressing the desire to help:

Figure 4–2. Young slave reading the Bible to children outside a cabin (collection of the New York Historical Society).

Figure 4–3. Slaves dancing during a rare free moment (courtesy of the Library of Congress, LC-USZ62–30960).

Do you want to live with me?
I would give them food and water.
I would give them a jacket.
Let's build an Underground Railroad.
Come back into the new world with me.

Several of the groups struggled with a question about what they had in common with the children who were slaves. The preservice teachers had to do some scaffolding to help them get started. After the class, they showed me what the students had written. A few wrote that they had nothing in common with the children, who were slaves, but others listed ways in which they were alike:

I have the same skin color.
We are people.
We both have to work.
We play outside.
We have some friends.
They like to dance and sing and so do I.
I want my dad, too. (in response to a recollection of a former slave about his father being sold)
We both have a family. (in response to a photograph of a slave family)
We both feel slavery is dumb.
I feel scared sometimes in my neighborhood about getting robbed or hurt.
We both feel sad.

The preservice teachers in this fifth-grade classroom were reading from the shortened version of the first autobiography of Frederick Douglass, *Escape from Slavery: The Boyhood of Frederick Douglass in His Own Words*. Using this book is a good way for students to begin the process of "meeting" specific children who were slaves and discovering what life was like for them. Douglass describes his childhood and youth in slavery, including his first experience of learning to read, quoted at the beginning of this chapter. In her foreword, Coretta Scott King calls Douglass' autobiography "one of the best firsthand descriptions of slavery ever written" (Douglass 1994, viii). Older students may wish to read selections in the original version, *Narrative of the Life of Frederick Douglass, An American Slave, Written by Himself*.

Another classic of slave literature is Harriet Jacobs' autobiography, *Incidents in the Life of a Slave Girl*. You could read selections about Harriet's childhood to your students. *I Was Born a Slave*, a juvenile biography by Jennifer Fleischner (1997), based on Harriet's autobiography, could be read by older students. Harriet had a kind mistress who died, then she was sold to a cruel couple. Harriet recalls the first time she was punished:

> It was in the month of February. My grandmother had taken my old shoes, and replaced them with a new pair. I needed them; for several inches of snow had fallen, and it still continued to fall. When I walked through Mrs. Flint's room, their creaking grated harshly on her refined nerves. . . . "Take them off," said she; "and if you put them on again, I'll throw them into the fire." I took them off. . . . She then sent me a long distance, on an errand. As I went through the snow, my bare feet tingled. That night I was very hoarse. (Jacobs 2000, 1861, 19)

Oral histories of former slaves were collected by the Library of Congress in 1936 through the Federal Writers' Project. Belinda Hurmence selected some interviews of people who were children when slavery ended in 1865 for her book, *Slavery Time When I Was Chilllun* (1997). Students reading these interviews will find descriptions of living conditions, food, games, hardships, mistreatment, and what it was like to finally be free.

Many accounts of former slaves recall beatings, other mistreatment, and the trauma of being sold as a child or having their family members sold.

> A single word from the white men was enough—against all our wishes, prayers, and entreaties—to sunder forever the dearest friends, dearest kindred, and strongest ties known to human beings. If any one thing in my experience, more than another, served to . . . fill me with unutterable loathing of slaveholders, it was their base ingratitude to my poor old grandmother. She had served my old master faithfully from his youth to old age. . . . She had rocked him in infancy, attended him in childhood, served him through life, and at his death . . . closed his eyes forever. She was nevertheless left . . . a slave in the hands of strangers; and in their hands she saw her children, . . . divided, like so many sheep. (Douglass, 1994, 17)

Mary Prince, who was born into slavery, describes being sold when she was twelve. Her mother had to take her and her sisters to the slave market.

> The *vendue* (auction) master, who was to offer us for sale like sheep or cattle . . . asked my mother which was the eldest. She said nothing, but pointed to me. . . . I was then put up to sale. . . . I then saw my sisters led forth, and sold to different owners; so that we had not the sad satisfacton of being partners in bondage. When the sale was over, my mother hugged and kissed us, and mourned over us. . . . It was a sad parting; one went one way, one another, and our poor mammy went home with nothing. (Prince 1988, 62–63 in Stepto 1994, 31–32)

Students usually have questions about the kinds of work required of children who were slaves. Sylviane Diouf, in *Growing Up in Slavery*, explains the chores of younger children and the labors of older children. Some recollections of former slaves give details of the work they did as children. Venture Smith was ordered to perform increasingly harder tasks as he grew older:

> The first of the time of living at my master's own place, I was pretty much employed in the house at carding wool and other household business. . . . I then began to have hard tasks imposed on me. Some of these were to pound four bushels of ears of corn every night in a barrel for the poultry, or be rigorously punished. At other seasons of the year I had to card wool until a very late hour. These tasks I had to perform when I was about nine years old. (Porter 1995, 546 in Bolden 2001, 19)

In Union Parish, Louisiana, Mary Island washed dishes when she was four and cooked when she was six.

> While the other hands was working in the field I carried water. We had to cook out in the yard on an old skillet and lid, so you see I had to tote brush and bark and roll up little logs such as I could to keep the fire from one time of cooking to the other. . . . When I got to be seven years old I was cutting sprouts almost like a man and when I was eight I could pick one hundred pounds of cotton. (Berlin 1998, 95 in Bolden 2001, 33)

Students are interested in the food, dress, and housing of children who were slaves. Diouf describes the way these children lived and includes quotes from former slaves in her book. In his autobiography (1994), Douglass tells how he suffered with cold and hunger as a young child:

> I suffered much from hunger, but much more from cold. . . . I was kept almost naked—no shoes, no stockings, no jacket, no trousers, nothing on but a coarse tow linen shirt, reaching only to my knees. I had no bed. . . . I used to steal a bag which was used for carrying corn to the mill. I would crawl into this bag, and there sleep on the cold, damp, clay floor, with my head in and feet out. My feet have been so cracked with the frost, that the pen with which I am writing might be laid in the gashes. (Douglass 1994, 8)

Robert Shepherd and other children ate at a long trough in the yard:

> For dinner, us had peas or some other sort of veg'tables, and corn bread. Aunt Viney crumbled up dat bread in de trough and poured de veg'tables and pot-licker over it. Den, she blowed the horn and chillun come a-runnin' from evvy which away. . . . At nights, she crumbled de corn bread in de trough and poured buttermilk over it. (Mellon 1998, 38 in Bolden 2001, 35)

Some students who read about the lives of children as slaves wonder if they ever had any fun or any toys. Slaves had very little free time, of course. Bolden notes that many former slaves could not recall anything but work. Sylviane Diouf devotes a chapter to the leisure activity of the children who were slaves. During precious free time, adults who remembered being free in Africa told the children stories of life there. Singing, dancing, making music on homemade instruments, and telling African tales featuring animals entertained them. Children made rag or corn-husk dolls and clay marbles. Some former slaves had fond memories of rare free times. James Bolton, who was a slave in Georgia, recalled blowing quills. "Quills was a row of whistles made out of reeds. . . . Every whistle in the row was a different tone and you could play any kind of tune you wants if you had a good row of quills" (Killion 1973, 25 in Diouf 2001, 54). Manda Boggan, who was enslaved in Mississippi, remembered how she played. "Us made play houses under the big oak trees. Us raked up big piles of leaves for beds, and made rag-dolls . . . and dresses and hats out of leaves pinned together with pine straws. Then us played run and ketch games us made up" (Berlin 1998, 41 in Bolden 2001, 31).

Students are sometimes surprised to find out that some children growing up in slavery did manage to learn to read and write. The stories of how they did so are fascinating—they were determined to become literate in spite of the risk of being punished if their owners found out. Some, like Phillis Wheatley (Figure 4–4), were more fortunate. Her owners helped her get an education. She was kidnapped in Senegal at age seven, taken to Boston, and bought by Susannah Wheatley, the wife of a wealthy merchant. The Wheatleys treated Phillis like a member of their family and encouraged her talent for writing poetry. Her first poem was published when she was twelve. Later a book of her poems, most written when she was a teenager, sold well in both England and America. Phillis became free when the Wheatleys died (Hoose 2001).

Another young captive who also learned to read and write managed to buy his freedom when he was twenty-one. Olaudah Equiano, the son of a tribal leader, was born in Nigeria and kidnapped by slave traders when he was eleven. He suffered on the slave ship and was sold to a British naval officer, who took him to England. When he was sold later to a Quaker in Philadelphia, Olaudah worked for six years to buy his freedom. Some students would be interested in reading his own words about how he accomplished this, and they can: *The Interesting Narratives of the Life of Olaudah Equiano, or Gustavus Vassa, the African, Written by Himself* describes the horrors of being kidnapped as a child and working as a slave. The book, which was one of the first written in English by an African, became a bestseller (Hoose 2001).

Some children traveled on the Underground Railroad, usually with parents escaping north, to freedom. Ann Maria Weems was only fifteen when she fled from Maryland and was unaccompanied by an adult guide. A wealthy Quaker lawyer and the leader of the Pennsylvania Anti-Slavery Society helped her escape by disguising her as a male carriage driver and arranging for her to go to different

Figure 4–4. Phillis Wheatley, whose first poem was published at age twelve (courtesy of the Library of Congress, LC-USZ62–40054).

points along the Underground Railroad to get to Canada (Fradin 2000; Hoose 2001).

Children whose parents were conductors on the Underground Railroad sometimes helped to hide, feed, and transport slaves. One of these was Allen Jay, whose Quaker parents were secret conductors living in Randolph, Ohio. His recollection of helping one particular fugitive slave is an exciting story and can be found in Phillip Hoose's *We Were There, Too!* Marlene Brill (1993) tells his story very simply for younger children in *Allen Jay and the Underground Railroad*. Another young conductor in Ohio, Lucinda Wilson, also had the job of looking out for runaways and assisting them. In one particular incident, she hid two young girls in her room, one in a clothes hamper and the other in her nightclothes in bed with her, just before bounty hunters burst into her room (Hoose 1993).

Child Labor

Although they weren't slaves, many children in poor families worked from dawn to dark, Monday through Saturday, in mills, factories, coal mines, and fields during the Industrial Revolution and into the first part of the twentieth century. Most of them had little, if any, chance to go to school, and they suffered from the unhealthy conditions and dangers of the places in which they worked. Many of our students may not be aware that child labor is a part of American history. The students in a fifth-grade class I worked with had trouble believing that parents would allow their children to work such long hours in unsafe places, even if the families were poor. They were very interested in finding out more about the lives of these children. I presented some background information and read descriptions and firsthand accounts of children's work experiences. Then the classroom teacher and I introduced Lewis Hine's photographs of scenes of child labor (Figures 4–5 through 4–9) and gave each group of students a photograph to examine, accompanied by a list of questions. We had planned to rotate the photographs so that each group would be able to examine three of them, but when we attempted to stop and have the students share their responses, they protested. They wanted to see all of the photographs, and even asked if we had more. They were really fascinated and involved, so we continued until everyone had seen all of the photographs. An aide in the classroom became involved with a group studying a photograph of children in coal mines. She described the stories her grandfather had told her about working in the Pennsylvania mines. This teaching session became a meaningful experience for all of us in the room.

Later, as the teacher and I read the students' answers to the questions about the photographs, we were impressed with the thoughtfulness and insight shown in

Figure 4–5. Spinner in a cotton mill, North Pownal, Vermont, 1910 (courtesy of the Library of Congress, LC USZ62–12880).

some of their responses. For example, in answer to why they thought the photographs were taken about a hundred years ago, one group looking at a factory photograph noted how the people were dressed, that the photo was black-and-white, and that the machinery did not look safe for children to use. Another group, looking at children who had fallen asleep in a night school because they had worked all day, wrote, "The school had children of all ages in one room and they don't have that now-a-days." Workplace dangers were a concern of some groups. One group wrote that children could get cut because of glass in a glass factory, sharp machinery in a mill, or being barefoot. Another group described some of the dangers as getting sick, falling, or getting dehydrated from working in the sun all day.

When the students wrote about how they thought the children might have felt about working in these places, they were able to give good reasons for their thinking. One group said the children might have felt sad because their families were poor and glad because they could help their families. Another said they may have felt proud because they were getting money and scared because of the things they worked with. One wrote that the children were mad because they had to use flame in the glass factory and sad and bored because they had to work all the time.

The classroom teacher and I were especially interested in reading the fifth graders' responses to the question "If you could step into this photograph, what questions would you ask the children?" We were surprised by some of the answers. We had expected that the students might ask "How does it feel to work all day?" and "How does it feel to not have any free time?" and many did ask these questions. However, some, instead of asking questions, wanted to do something to help the child laborers. One wrote, "I would take this little girl out and get her new clothes." Another said, "I would give him advice to get out of that place and come with me." This indicated to us that the students had really connected with these historical children and saw them as being real. Their responses were similar to the reactions of a fifth-grade class in a different school who looked at photographs of children who were slaves. The students in both classes wanted to go back in time and help the young people they saw.

The photographs used in this fifth-grade lesson are from the Jackdaw collection *Child Labor, the Shame of the Nation* and Russell Freedman's *Kids at Work: Lewis Hine and the Crusade Against Child Labor* (1994). Many other books on child labor contain photographs that could be used in the classroom.

In addition to studying photographs, these historical children can become "real" to our students through reading or hearing the actual accounts of children who were laborers during this period of our history. These, along with the first-hand accounts of adults who reported on child labor, are readily available.

When Samuel Slater started the first mill in America in Rhode Island in 1790, he hired nine children to run it. They were the first factory workers in

Figure 4–6. Replacing bobbins in a cotton mill (courtesy of the Library of Congress, LC-USZ62–23944).

Figure 4–7. Young coal mine workers and mule in Grafton, West Virginia, 1908 (Lewis Hine Collection, Albin O. Kuhn Library, University of Maryland, Baltimore County, no. 157).

America. These seven boys and two girls, who ranged in age from seven to twelve, worked fourteen hours a day, six days a week. One of these children was ten-year-old Smith Wilkinson, who would later become Slater's brother-in-law. In *We Were There, Too!* Phillip Hoose lists the names of the other eight children and describes their contributions in the early days of the mill. Samuel Slater himself was only twenty-two when he started the mill. He had begun work at age fourteen as an apprentice in a British mill.

American textile mills employed more than a million children by 1830. Lucy Larcom and Harriet Hanson, who began working in one of the Lowell, Massachusetts, mills at age eleven, wrote about their lives. Both girls' fathers had died and their mothers struggled to support families by keeping a boarding house where mill workers lived. In *A New England Girlhood: Outlined from Memory*, Lucy describes her thoughts and feelings about her days in the mill.

> I heard it said one day, in a distressed tone, "The children will have to leave school and go into the mill." . . . I was then between eleven and twelve years old. . . . the feeling had already come to me, that I was the one too many in the overcrowded family nest. . . . So I went to my first day's work in the mill. . . . The novelty of it made it seem easy, and it really was not hard, just to change the bobbins on the spinning frames every three quarters of an hour or so, with half a dozen other little girls who were doing the same thing. . . . And for a little while it was only a new amusement. . . . I never cared much for machinery. The buzzing and hissing and whizzing of pulleys and rollers and spindles and flyers around me often grew tiresome. . . . It was not . . . the right sort of life for a child. . . . The little money I could earn—one dollar a week, besides the price of my board—was needed in the family, and I must return to the mill. . . . (Larcom 1986, 153–155)

Lucy eventually went west with her sister and brother-in-law and became a teacher, poet, and writer. In her narrative poem about Lowell, *An Idyl of Work*, she captured her boredom with her work in the mill:

> When I first
> Learned to doff bobbins, I just thought it play.
> But when you do the same thing twenty times,—
> A hundred times a day,—it is so dull! (1970, 49)

Harriet Hanson (Robinson) tells about her childhood in the cotton mill in *Loom and Spindle, or Life Among the Early Mill Girls*. She writes, "I can see myself now, racing down the alley, between the spinning-frames, carrying in front of me a bobbin-box bigger than I was" (Robinson 1976, 19). Her greatest hardship at first was being on duty nearly fourteen hours each day. Harriet and the other girls had sympathy for the English factory children they had heard about, who were whipped and treated badly by overseers. Harriet tried to get an education:

I had been to school quite constantly until I was nearly eleven years of age, and then, after going into the mill, I went to some of the evening schools that had been established. . . . Some of these schools were devoted to special studies. I went to a geography school, where the lessons were repeated in unison in a monotonous sing-song tone, like this: "Lake Winnipeg! Lake Winnipeg! Lake Titicaca! Lake Titicaca!" (25)

Harriet describes the *Lowell Offering*, a magazine written, edited, and published by Lowell mill girls from 1840–1845, expressing her pride that at the time, there were only three other women editors in America. Harriet, Lucy, and other mill girls contributed poems, stories, and articles about their lives and dreams to

Figure 4–8. Young driver and his mule working in a mine in Pittston, Pennsylvania, 1911 (Lewis Hine Collection, Albin O. Kuhn Library, University of Maryland, Baltimore County, no. 1921).

this literary magazine. The March 2001 issue of *Cobblestone* is about the mill girls and includes an article about this magazine. When Charles Dickens visited Lowell in 1842, he read the *Lowell Offering* and was very impressed with the writing ability of the mill girls. Dickens himself at age twelve had to work in a shoe-polish factory in London, pasting labels in an old building overrun with rats.

Older students might find Lucy's and Harriet's writings interesting not only because of the details they provide about working in the mills, but also because they describe their home lives, activities, and amusements. For younger students, you could read aloud from these books or from quotations about child labor included in juvenile literature.

Rose Cohen was twelve when she began working in a New York City sweatshop. She grew up in a Russian village. Her father, who had taught her how to sew, sent for her after he had settled in New York so that she could help him make enough money to bring the rest of the family to America. In her autobiography, *Out of the Shadow,* Rose describes how she felt when she first began working in a shop sewing coats:

> From this hour a hard life began for me. [The boss] refused to employ me except by the week. He paid me three dollars and for this he hurried me from early until late. . . . He was never satisfied. . . . Late at night when the people would stand up and begin to fold their work away . . . he would come over with still another coat. . . . I understood that he was taking advantage of me because I was a child. And now that it was dark in the shop except for the low single gas jet over my table and the one over his . . . , and there was no one to see, more tears fell on the sleeve lining than there were stitches in it. (Cohen 1995, 112 in Hoose 2001, 167)

Nine-year-old Joseph Miliauskas began working for a coal mine as a breaker boy when his family emigrated from Lithuania in 1900. He sat all day on a bench picking out refuse as coal flowed down chutes, covering him and the other boys with coal dust.

> It was up to us to watch and pick the slate [rock that couldn't be burned] out. We had to throw it to the side and let the clean coal go down. The boss was behind us with a broom and if he caught you slipping up and letting some slate come down, boy, you'd get it in the back with a broom. . . . [My] second day [on the job] my fingers were all cut up and bleeding. . . . [After] you're there two or three weeks, your fingers get hardened up. No more blood. You get used to it. (Hoose 2001, 168–169)

In spite of the terrible working conditions, the boys managed to have some fun. Joseph describes how they ate lunch quickly so that they could play tag in complete darkness in the mine. "We'd go over the machinery and around it. . . . We'd get to know it like a bunch of rats" (Bartoletti 1996, 21, 170). When he became a

Figure 4–9. Young worker in an Alexandria, Virginia, glass factory, 1911. The comments in the bubbles are samples of what students said when asked, "If you could talk to this boy, what would you say to him or ask him?" (Courtesy of the Library of Congress, LC-US262-10960.)

"nipper," his job was to open and close a door from one part of the mine to the other. He amused himself by feeding crumbs to the rats and making friends with the mules hauling coal cars.

Growing Up in Coal Country, by Susan Bartoletti (1996), is an excellent book for students to use in discovering what life was like for children working in the mines. She describes the mining process and its dangers; gives interesting accounts of how mules and birds helped the miners; and includes the voices of children, men, and women. The stories of the tricks the boys played on cruel bosses, ghosts in the mines, superstitions, and mule boys making pets out of their mules would be fascinating to students. There are also stories of children bravely helping others in dangerous situations. Martin Crahan was a twelve-year-old mule driver. When there was a fire, he had the chance to ride the cage out of the mine to safety. Instead, he went back to warn the other nineteen miners about the fire. He died next to his mule. William McKinney let the miners kill and eat his pet mule to save their lives when they were trapped underground for nine days.

The photograph of the boys with the mule (Figure 4–7) was probably taken when they had just come up from the mine. This photo and the one of the boy leading a mule in the mine (Figure 4–8) can motivate students to discuss the dangers these boys faced, what it was like to be underground all day, and the boys' relationships with their mules.

Children Striking

When the students we were teaching in the fifth-grade classroom had finished examining the photographs, the classroom teacher and I asked if anyone thought the children had done anything to improve their situations. No one thought that they had. We then told them that children had participated in and even helped lead strikes to try to get fewer hours and better wages. This seemed to elicit feelings of admiration and even reassurance that children had been able to take these actions.

In *Kids on Strike* (1999), Susan Bartoletti tells stories of children involved in strikes. The one about the New York newsboys, or "newsies," who in 1899 took on the owners of the *New York Journal* and the *New York World*, William Hearst and Joseph Pulitzer, is incredible. The boys organized and refused to deliver their papers when the price they had to pay for a bundle of papers was increased. When sales dropped, Hearst and Pulitzer offered a deal that was acceptable to the newsies.

Many boys working in coal mines joined the United Mine Workers, paid union dues, and attended weekly meetings just like the older miners did.

Bartoletti (1996) describes how effectively the young mule drivers persuaded miners to join the union. If a miner was not a member, some mule boys refused to deliver the empty coal cars they needed to take their coal above ground. The boys also supported each other by going on strike if other boys were treated unfairly.

In 1836, Harriet Hanson took an active part when a strike was planned at the mill where she worked. On the day of the strike, the girls and women in the upper rooms left first. In Harriet's room, the girls hesitated. But eleven-year-old Harriet said, "I don't care what you do, I am going to turn out, whether any one else does or not." She walked out into the mill yard and then looked behind her. She later wrote in her autobiography, "As I looked back at the long line that followed, I was more proud than I have ever been since at any success I may have achieved" (Robinson 1976, 52).

In July 1828, one of the first recorded children's strikes took place at a mill in Patterson, New Jersey, when the owners moved the noon meal to one o'clock. The children wanted the earlier meal time restored and a shorter workday. After the third day of the strike, the owners granted their request for the noon meal, but not the one for a shorter workday (Bartoletti 1999, 22).

In addition to participating in strikes, children gave their testimonies. Some of these testimonies are found in the Cobblestone series *Child Labor in America: Teaching with Primary Sources*. Fourteen-year-old Camella Teoli, John Boleder, Charles Dhooghe, and other children working in the mills of Lawrence, Massachusetts, testified before Congress in the early 1900s about their working conditions, pay, and injuries.

Some of the working children in the North were also concerned about those who were slaves in the South. Girls in the textile mills knew that slaves had grown the cotton they were spinning and weaving, and therefore signed many petitions against slavery (Selden 1997). Lucy Larcom expressed her feelings later in her narrative poem "An Idyl of Work," published in 1875:

> When I've thought what soil the cotton-plant
> We weave is rooted in, what waters it—
> The blood of souls in bondage—I have felt
> That I was sinning against the light to stay
> And turn the accursed fibre into cloth. (Larcom 1970, 135)

Children Laboring and in Bondage Today

Do you think child labor is happening today?, the fifth-grade teacher and I asked the students participating in our child labor lesson. The students said "no," but then one reconsidered. He said it could be happening in other countries that were poor, but not here. We asked, Why not here? Some of their answers were "People have more money," "we have more technology," "we think about children in a different way," "we have laws," and "we have more safety." We then discussed what's happening in some countries today and talked about the long hours and unhealthy working conditions of children in migrant families in the United States.

It is shocking to find out that from ten to twenty million children work as bonded laborers in our world today (Parker 1998). Being a bonded laborer is similar to being a slave. Children are sold to employers who loan money to their parents. The children work until the loan is paid back, which in many cases can never happen. There are some excellent books to use in helping students to understand child labor and child slavery today, through which they can meet some of these children. In *Child Slavery in Modern Times*, by Shirlee Newman (2000), students can view photographs of children working in brick factories, steel mills, gold mines, stone-crushing plants, carpet factories, and sporting-goods factories, and see children who are domestic slaves, and even camel jockeys. Newman clearly explains why and how this happens. Her book contains interviews with children and young people who describe their work and their feelings, including children in the United States who work as field laborers or in sweatshops where labor laws are ignored.

Stolen Dreams: Portraits of Working Children is by David Parker, M.D., who reminds me of a modern-day Lewis Hine. He became interested in photographing working children when he was doing research on how work affects young people, and the book has black-and-white photographs on almost every page. Parker explains the children's situations and includes quotations from children around the world. Readers are introduced to thirteen-year-old Doi, who makes leather handbags in a factory in Bangkok, Thailand:

> My father died and my mother just didn't have enough money to feed all my brothers and sisters, so that's why I came. . . . What I really miss is games. We don't have any time to play. . . . I don't understand why we can't have some time in the evening to play. (Parker 1998, 71–72)

Iqbal Masih, a remarkable child, is a wonderful role model for our students. His intelligence, resiliency, and concern for others are amazing. In his short life, he brought the world's attention to children in bondage. Iqbal, born in Pakistan, was sold when he was four years old to a carpet factory owner for 600 rupees (twelve dollars). He was chained to a loom during working hours. At age ten he escaped, and with the help of the Bonded Labor Liberation Front, started school. He began to help other children be free too. Students can read about his life in *Iqbal Masih and the Crusaders Against Child Slavery* by Susan Kuklin (1998).

The students at Broad Meadows Middle School in Quincy, Massachusetts, got to meet Iqbal when he came to Boston to receive a Reebok Human Rights Youth in Action Award. The Reebok Foundation arranged for him to visit the school so that he could get to know American children (Figure 4–10). In Ron Adams' seventh-grade classroom, the students had been studying the origins of the Civil War and the Industrial Revolution. When Iqbal walked into their classroom, he said, "I understand that you are studying slavery in the United States. I'm here to tell you it is still alive" (Kuklin 1998, 79). He then described his life. Unfortunately, four and a half months later, after he returned to Pakistan, the death threats that he had been receiving became a reality: Iqbal was shot on April 16, 1995. He was only twelve years old.

Lost Futures: The Problem of Child Labor, a videotape and teacher's guide published by the American Federation of Teachers (AFT) (1999), is an excellent resource to use with students. It begins with a brief history of child labor and then features the plight of children in oppressive labor today, both in and outside of

Figure 4–10. Iqbal Masih, formerly a child laborer in Pakistan, visiting Ron Adams' seventh-grade class at Broad Meadows Middle School in Quincy, Massachusetts (courtesy of Ron Adams).

the United States. Iqbal's visit to Broad Meadows Middle School is on the video, and students in Ron Adams' classroom are interviewed about how his visit affected them.

Our students can be inspired and moved by the stories of children, both present and past, in slavery and oppressive labor. They can also make connections between past and present, as the seventh-grade students at Broad Meadows Middle School did. Kuklin describes the effect of Iqbal's visit:

> Iqbal's talk left the students breathless. The lessons of the past had been ignored. Pakistan was a developing country, just like the United States had been more than a hundred years ago. Developing countries were making the same mistakes the United States and England made. (Kuklin 1998, 80)

Using the Resources

Each time I teach or observe teachers using photographs of historical children, I am intrigued by the students' responses and intense interest. The same thing happens when students read historical accounts. Photographs or stories used alone can provide a meaningful experience, but using the two together is powerful. In both classes just described, using these two types of primary sources simultaneously enabled the students to make more connections with the children they learned about and to empathize more deeply with their situations. They were able to comprehend that they were studying real young people, just like them, who happened to live in the past or in another part of the world. In working with historical source materials, students grow in the ability to meet the NCSS performance expectation of developing "critical sensitivities such as empathy and skepticism regarding attitudes, values, and behaviors of people in different historical contexts" (NCSS 1994, 34).

Analyzing Primary Sources

Asking open questions helps students use sources effectively. The fifth-graders used some of the same questions to analyze the photographs of slavery and child labor:

1. Look carefully at each section of the photograph and list what you see.
2. What clues in this photograph tell you when it was taken?
3. What things can you find out about this child or these children by looking at this photograph? Why?
4. What do you have in common with this child or these children?

5. If you could step into this photograph and talk to this child or these children, what would you say? What questions would you ask?
6. How do you think this child or these children feel? Why?
7. How do you feel about the way this child or these children have to live? Why?

The following additional questions were on the guide for the child labor photographs:

8. What do you think this child or these children might be thinking about while working in this place? Why?
9. What dangers might this child or these children face by working in this place? Why?
10. How would you feel if you were working with this child or these children in this place? Why?

The fifth-grade lesson on slavery also included a sheet to use for analyzing the accounts of former slaves. Students were asked to do the following:

1. List what you discovered about the life of this child by reading what he or she said.
2. How do you feel about how they had to live as slaves?
3. If you could talk to this child, what questions would you ask? What would you tell him or her?
4. List what you have in common with this child.

Questions 4, 5, 6, 7, 8, and 10 for the photographs and 2, 3, and 4 for the accounts are designed to help students make connections with children who were slaves or laborers. Some students may need a little scaffolding to respond to the question of what they have in common with something other than being near the same age. You might expand on the question by asking students to think about needs, wants, families, friends, feelings, and other aspects of their lives. It is important to explore the questions on commonality thoroughly. Milton Meltzer emphasizes that students "can find common bonds with people far off in time and space, recognizing in them our common humanity, while understanding the differences that may separate us" (Meltzer 1993, 29). Questions 5, 6, 7, and 10 help students connect with children in the past on personal and feeling levels. "Being able to take the perspective of people in the past is a requirement for meaningful historical understanding," according to Levstik and Barton (1997, 114), and that is just what these questions help students to do.

Telling students to look carefully at each section of a photograph helps increase their observation skills. They should examine photos as a historian would. When the classroom teacher and I taught the child labor lesson, we noted that a number of the students were exceptionally thorough about doing this. They even noticed some details that I had overlooked, in spite of the many times I have seen the photographs. For example, one student saw the face of an animal in the lower-right corner of the photo of the girl leaning on a spinning machine (Figure 4–5). I had never noticed this. Considerable debate ensued about whether the face belonged to a monkey, a rat, or a cat, and the students suggested what it might be doing there. A magnifying glass would have helped us examine the photo more closely, so in the future, I'll provide some when students analyze photographs.

As teachers we know the importance of providing enough time for students to examine and analyze photographs and accounts in-depth and to record their reactions. It is also essential for them to share the results of their work. Information to share can be placed on graphic organizers like those in Figures 4–11 through 4–13. These visual displays can help students develop generalizations about what they discovered about historical children and their lives by working with primary sources.

Writing Creative Responses to Primary Sources

The students' responses to the other questions could be followed up in a number of ways. For example, what they write about how they feel about the children's situations could be expressed by writing a pretend letter to one of the children. What they would say to the children if they could talk to them might be written inside cartoon bubbles arranged around a photograph on a poster (Figure 4–9).

Lives of Children Who Were Slaves					
Food	*Clothing*	*Living Conditions*	*Work*	*Education*	*Auctions*

Figure 4–11.

Child Labor			
Place of Work	*What They Do*	*Dangers/ Conditions*	*Hours*
Mines			
Mills			
Fields			
Factories			

Figure 4–12.

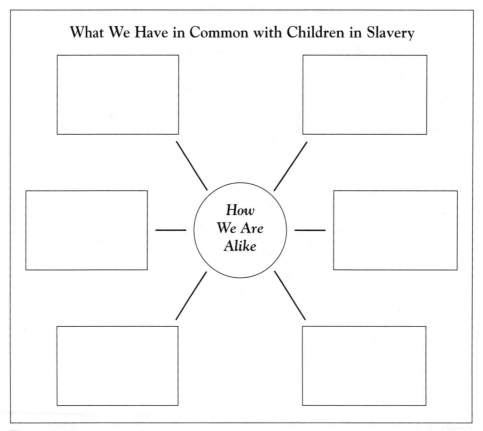

What We Have in Common with Children in Slavery

How We Are Alike

Figure 4–13.

Any questions students ask the children could be answered by other students pretending to be the children in the photographs.

Students reading about Phillis Wheatley, a slave who had her first poem published at age twelve, or the mill girls who wrote essays, fiction, and poetry for the *Lowell Offering*, might be inspired by their example and express their feelings about slavery and child labor through poetry. In *Nonfiction Matters*, Stephanie Harvey states that the teacher of a fifth-grade bilingual class found that students who are learning English often prefer poetry because it is "convention free and at its best when short, crisp, and expressive . . ." (1998, 175). This teacher was impressed with the striking poetry some of her students wrote. You might suggest that your students write poems from the perspective of a child who was a slave or who labored in a mill, factory, or mine. To help your students focus on the children's feelings, display their responses to the questions about what the children may have been feeling or thinking and reread selections from the primary accounts students read. Excerpts from some of Phyllis Wheatley's or Lucy Larcom's poems could provide further inspiration. Displaying the photographs your students looked at and playing appropriate background music can help establish a climate for writing.

Some of your students might be interested in writing essays, stories, poems, or plays similar to those in the *Lowell Offering*. *Children at Work: Researching American History* (Deitch 2000a) reproduces an essay written by Almira, a Lowell mill girl, that is a a good example of what the magazine published. Almira's essay includes a conversation between two girls about the advantages and disadvantages of mill work. Students could publish their own issue of the *Lowell Offering* by putting their writings together and making a cover similar to the one on the original magazine.

The descriptions of strikes in Susan Bartoletti's *Kids on Strike!* are so vivid that your students could use them to write news articles about children participating in or even leading strikes in the mines, mills, factories, and newspaper industry. For photographs to accompany the articles the students could take pictures of each other dressed as different kinds of workers. For props, they could make signs similar to those shown in photographs of strikes.

Designing and Using Simulations

The effectiveness of using simulations or experiential exercises as a teaching strategy was reconfirmed for me recently. Every year I present workshops at both the NCSS conference and the Northeast Regional Conference for the Social Studies (NERC) on some aspect of children in history. At the 2003 NERC workshop, several of the participants were coordinators of social studies for middle schools. We all shared ideas for using primary sources by or about children in history. One of the coordinators explained how she had used simulation in teaching about child labor at her school. The teachers arranged desks in three rows to simulate a factory line, then had the students do a repetitive task (folding paper a certain way, threading needles, etc.) quickly while a tape played machine sounds. An overseer for each row told them to work faster and faster. Afterward, the students wrote about how they felt and what they thought it would be like to do something so boring thirteen hours a day, six days a week.

Another of the teachers at the NERC workshop described taking his class to a closet in the basement of the school and reading accounts of what it was like to be in the hold of a ship while they sat crowded in the semidarkness. That prompted the idea that the same kind of thing could be done to simulate working in a mine. A teacher could simulate the work of breaker boys in a coal mine by having students sit three in a row behind each other, as those boys did, and pass small boxes of stones from student to student while each tries to quickly remove stones that don't fit certain criteria.

We all agreed that such simulations cannot even begin to approximate what real people suffered, but they can help students begin to try to view life and history from perspectives other than their own. Joyce and Weil (1996) state that simulations, including both the activity and follow-up discussion, "nurture and instruct a variety of educational outcomes, including concepts . . . ; and empathy" (362). The Teachers' Curriculum Institute's *History Alive! Engaging All Learners in the Diverse Classroom* (1994) has a chapter on how to use experiential exercises or simulations in the classroom and explains the benefits of doing so. Three benefits are particularly relevant to understanding children in slavery and child labor: First, simulations and experimental exercises are memorable and motivating. The teachers in the NERC workshop talked about how students recall how meaningful such experiences were for them. Second, when students learn historical concepts through simulations, they use what Howard Garner (1993) calls the intrapersonal and body-kinesthetic intelligences: They become conscious of their own feelings about what the historical children experienced and use their bodies to understand what it was like for the children to do repetitive tasks under great pressure to produce. Third, high-level concepts become more concrete when students experience them on a feeling level.

The *History Alive!* chapter on experiential exercises has helpful guidelines for teachers, such as communicating your expectations and directions clearly. Since the experiences are unusual, students must know their purpose and the procedures and rules to follow. It's essential that you debrief after the activity, because students need to talk about their feelings and verbally make connections to history. Then use discussion to help your students understand how the simulation experience is different from historical reality. For example, after doing the repetitive activity you might ask the students what feelings they experienced, what about the task was difficult, and how they coped with the repetition. You would then explain that what they did doesn't even come close to the boredom, dangers, and hardship the historical children faced. Failing to make the difference clear would trivialize the historical children's experiences (Teachers' Curriculum Institute 1994).

Visiting and Creating Museums

Visiting a museum is another way to help students make connections with children who were slaves or in oppressive labor. I live in Rhode Island and have visited both Slater Mill Historic Site in Pawtucket, Rhode Island, and Lowell National Historic Park in Lowell, Massachusetts, where I felt as if I had traveled back in time to when children were working in these mills. I still remember the roar when they started the machines inside one of the rooms at Lowell, even though they had given us cotton to put in our ears. I have also visited the Museum of Science and Industry in Chicago, which has a working replica of a coal mine. Riding down to the mine and seeing the displays helped me experience a little part of what it must have been like for children working in coal mines. These and many other museums have educational resources and programs for teachers to use. You might find a museum that's related to your class's historical explorations in your area.

Creating a museum display is a creative way for students to further their understanding of children in slavery or child labor, and to both share and demonstrate what they have learned. Teachers whose students create history museums can't say enough about the value of having students do this. Levstik and Barton, who devote a chapter of their book *Doing History* to creating a history museum, state that "teachers know they're on to something when students enjoy doing an assignment that does not come easily" (1997, 65). They describe how one teacher and her students created a museum. Peg Koetsch, who collaborates with the Smithsonian Institution in developing and implementing a national "Museum-in-Progress" program, states that "all the components of learning that the students experienced are woven together to form a central concept, which becomes the exhibition theme, and students' projects visually demonstrate their learning" (1994, 18). She cites other benefits based on her extensive experience: Creating an exhibit provides evidence of students' growth and gives closure to an in-depth study. Students are motivated to further inquiry because they know that others will view and try to understand their work, and that their learning is valued. Because of this they develop high standards for their work, standards that last even after the closing of an exhibit. "Teachers have noticed a dramatic increase in the students' expectations of what they can achieve and the quality of their work" (1994, 18).

Creating a museum display is an authentic follow-up to visiting an actual museum. A museum visit is the ideal way to introduce students to what is involved in the project. If it is not possible to take your students to a museum, prepare them for the project by inviting them to talk about their previous visits to museums, the different types of exhibits they saw, and their participation in any interactive exhibits. List what they say about different types of museum exhibits they've seen and interactive experiences they've had, then post the list in the classroom for them to refer to for ideas. Based on what they know about museums, your students may plan to do one or more of the following:

1. Paint a mural depicting the lives of children who were slaves or children who labored in factories, mills, mines, or fields. Write information about different parts of the mural on small posters and hang them under the relevant mural sections.

2. Create a three-dimensional scene in a large box to illustrate an account of the childhood of a former slave or laborer. Figures can be constructed out of clay, and your students can be resourceful in finding other materials to use. For example, to create a cotton field they could use bits of cotton balls and twigs. For a coal mine scene you could bring in fine gravel. Tape-record a student reading what the historical child said as if they were that child, then let each "museum" visitor listen to the tape when viewing the scene.

3. Display photographs of children who were slaves or child laborers in a "gallery" on the wall. Students can write their own captions for each photograph. They can find additional photographs by Lewis Hine on the Internet by going to the Archival Research Catalog database of the U.S. National Archives and Records Administration. (See "Teaching with Documents Lesson Plan: Photographs of Lewis Hine: Documentation of Child Labor," at *www.archives.gov/digital_classroom/lessons/ hine_photographs/hine_photographs.html.*

4. Create audiotapes of songs that children who were slaves, factory workers, or mine workers might have sung. Write information on small posters explaining the meaning of the songs of slaves in relation to the Underground Railroad, or the meaning of the songs of factory, mill, and mine workers. Visitors can start the tapes and read the background information. Relevant songs can be found in *Get on Board: The Story of the Underground Railroad,* by Jim Haskins (1993). The March 2001 issue

of *Cobblestone* includes a song of the Lowell mill girls. Your students may also wish to create and sing their own songs expressing something about the historical children's lives.

5. Make "artifacts" to display, such as a spindle from a mill. Write information about each one on a card and place it with the artifact.

6. Prepare to be tour guides for other classes, relatives, and community members when the "museum" opens.

The visual arts are a major part of student-created museum displays. Through painting and creating scenes, students can express their feelings and the feelings and thoughts of children who were slaves or who labored in mills, mines, and factories. Elliot Eisner emphasizes that the visual arts "provide the means through which meanings that are ineffable, but feelingful, can be expressed" (2002, 19). In *Art as Experience*, John Dewey states that "because the objects of art are expressive, they communicate. . . . Works of art are the only media of complete and unhindered communication . . . that can occur in a world full of gulfs and walls" (1934, 104–105). Students with differing abilities, backgrounds, and needs can communicate their feelings and the knowledge they gained about historical children by using the visual arts to move through these "gulfs and walls."

Understanding the Diversity in a Time Period

Keith Barton emphasizes that in helping students reach conclusions about the past, it is important that they understand the diversity of people's lives at a given time. They need to think about how people's lives might have been different depending on their ethnicity, economic background, sex, and location. "Understanding the range of life styles at a given time is a crucial component of historical understanding" (Barton 2001, 281). For example, to help your students see that children in the North were laboring in mills at the same time that children in the South were slaves, you might point out that some of the mill girls were concerned about working with cotton that slaves had produced. Comparing photographs and written accounts of children in different situations is another way to draw students' attention to this concept. If your students are finding out about the lives of poor children working as laborers in the nineteenth century, they might also look at the lives of children working as slaves and children living in middle-class and wealthy families in both the North and the South.

Comparing Primary Sources with Historical Fiction

You may wish to have your students compare primary sources by or about historical children with related historical fiction. Students sometimes do this on their own. When I was teaching child labor with the fifth-grade classroom teacher, several of the students began to make comparisons between the primary sources we used and *Lyddie*, a novel by Katherine Paterson. Other books related to child labor are *The Bobbin Girl*, by Emily McCully, *Hannah's Fancy Notions: A Story of Industrial New England*, by Pat Ross, and *Danger at the Breaker*, by Catherine Welch. *Minty: A Story of Young Harriet Tubman*, by Alan Schroeder, is a wonderful picture book for younger students. Mary Lyons' *Letters from a Slave Girl: The Story of Harriet Jacobs*, which is historical fiction, could be compared with Jacobs' real autobiography.

Children Taking Action Today

We can use Iqbal Masih's life and the stories of other children who have taken action against child labor and bondage in our world today to inspire our own students to find a way to help. Susan Kuklin's *Iqbal Masih and the Crusaders Against Child Slavery*, the American Federation of Teachers (AFT) videotape *Lost Futures*, and other sources tell stories about what young people have done to help other children around the world.

The seventh-grade students in the class that Iqbal visited at Broad Meadows Middle School were stunned when they heard of his death. They decided to fulfill the dream Iqbal had shared with them, of building a school in Pakistan for children who have been freed from child labor. Their story is in Kuklin's book, and they and their teacher, Ron Adams, are interviewed on the AFT videotape. These seventh graders accomplished the incredible feat of raising $147,000, and with that money a tiny five-room school opened in Pakistan. Your students may wish to visit the Broad Meadows Middle School website dedicated to Iqbal (*www.mirrorimage.com/iqbal/index.html*).

Lost Futures also includes an interview of a primary grade teacher and her students at P.S. 31 in Yonkers, New York, in which they talk about raising money to help children in Bangladesh, who had worked in a garment factory, go to school. The videotape and the accompanying teacher's guide offer other examples and a list of actions that students can take. These include writing letters to the editor of the local newspaper or to their senators or congressional representative, or writing to the head of a corporation about that company's production policies.

Foul Ball (*www.laborrights.org/projects/foulball/index.html*) and Rugmark (*www.rugmark.com*) are two programs that students can learn about and publicize in their schools and communities. The Rugmark label indicates that children have not been involved in making a hand-woven or hand-knotted rug. The Foul Ball label is placed on soccer balls so that buyers can be assured that they were not made by children. Students can refuse to buy and encourage others to refuse to buy clothes, carpets, toys, and sports equipment made by children.

A fifth-grade class in Aurora, Colorado, found out about slavery in Sudan, where children were kidnapped from northern Uganda and used as slaves in the northern Sudanese army. This class contacted the American Anti-Slavery Group and discovered that with the help of a Swiss human rights group they could buy a slave's freedom for fifty dollars. They worked to raise the money and publicized the need. Eventually they had five thousand dollars (Newman 2000, 21).

The books *Listen to Us: The World's Working Children*, by Jane Springer, and World Book's *Stand Up for Your Rights* have stories about children around the world who are laboring and in bondage, and accounts of young people who are working to change their situations. They include information about what our students can do. *Stand Up* was written by and for the young people of the world and is the result of a Peace Child International Project.

When twelve-year-old Craig Kielburger of Ontario, Canada, read about Iqbal Masih's death, he decided to take action. In 1995, he founded Free the Children, an activist group whose members range from age eight to age eighteen. Chapters in the United States, Australia, Chile, Brazil, India, Switzerland, and Sweden raise money for education centers and to buy sewing machines and cows so that families can earn money and not need their children to work. The teacher's guide with the *Lost Futures* video describes a Free the Children program to create health kits and school kits to be delivered to recently rescued child laborers. A classroom project like this could actively involve not just your students, but their families and neighbors as well. For more information, students can go to *www.freethechildren.org*. Older students can also read *Free the Children*, the book Craig wrote with Kevin Major.

Craig Kielburger traveled to Pakistan and India, where he visited children working in match, carpet, and glass factories. While he was there, he participated in a raid that freed bonded carpet weavers (Springer 1997, 91). His experiences have shown him that young people have the power to bring change, and that if we continue to educate people about a problem, a change will come. Our students can feel that power, too, as they connect with children, past and present, who believe in themselves. Craig captures what we hope our students will feel and understand when he says, "As young people, we have learned that knowledge is power. Child labor is a very complex issue but that is no excuse to ignore the problem. Who better than children to feel and understand the needs of other children?" (World Book 1998, 82). And, who better than our own students?

5

Children Participating in the Civil Rights and Women's Suffrage Movements

It was the high school, college, and elementary school young people who were in the front line of the school desegregation struggle. Lest it be forgotten, the opening of hundreds of schools . . . for the first time in history required . . . the moral and physical courage to face the challenges and, all too frequently, the mortal danger presented by mob resistance.

MARTIN LUTHER KING JR.

I did not go to school the day that I went on the march. . . . We started from Sixteenth Street Church. We always sang when we left the church. The singing. . . . gave you calmness and reassurance. We went down . . . by Kelly Ingram Park and marched. . . . Then the police put us in paddy wagons, and we went to Juvenile Hall. There were lots of kids, but I think I may have been the youngest. . . . I was nine. . . . I was in jail seven days.

AUDREY FAYE HENDRICKS, *who marched in one of the events in Birmingham, Alabama, that became known as the Children's Crusade (Levine 1993, 78–79)*

The value of young people's involvement in the Civil Rights movement is emphasized in the quotation above by Dr. Martin Luther King Jr. In this chapter, I invite you to meet some of the courageous girls and boys who made valuable contributions to the success of the civil rights movement. We will also become acquainted with some who took a stand on the Vietnam War and students' rights.

In a different historical period, we'll meet children involved in the women's suffrage movement by marching for voting rights and fair treatment for women.

The Civil Rights Movement

Imagine: You are in a classroom. In half of the room, chairs are arranged to represent seats on a bus, with one chair at the front where the "driver" is sitting. Students are improvising an event from the civil rights movement. The date is March 2, 1955. The location is Montgomery, Alabama. Several students are sitting in the back of the bus. A girl gets on and sits down in the middle of the bus, next to the window. You notice that all the riders on the bus are wearing black tags. The driver, who is wearing a white tag, pretends to drive and then stop. Students wearing white tags get on and begin to stare at the girl sitting in the middle of the bus. The driver asks the girl to move to the back of the bus, but she doesn't.

"I won't drive on until you get up," he tells her.

"Why don't you get up?" a student with a white tag says.

"She knows she has to get up," says another.

"She doesn't have to," a third student wearing a white tag says. "All she has to do is stay black and die."

"I'm getting the police," says the driver, and he leaves the bus.

A student playing the role of a traffic patrolman boards the bus and tells the girl to get up.

"No!" she says. "I have a constitutional right to sit here. I paid my fare."

Students acting as police get on the bus, knock the girl's books down, and lead her off the bus. They arrest her and take her away.

(Based on Claudette's account in Levine 1993, 23–24)

The dramatization ends. Then the students switch black and white tags, reverse roles, and enact the scene again. After the second enactment, the class discusses the feelings and insights that came to them as they participated.

What is the name of the person who refused to move? Most people would probably say Rosa Parks. But it was in December 1955 that Rosa Parks was arrested for refusing to give her seat on the bus to a white person. The event the students were role-playing happened nine months earlier, and the girl who refused to give up her seat was fifteen-year-old Claudette Colvin, not forty-two-year-old Rosa Parks. Why haven't more people heard about her? I hadn't until several years ago, when I read *Freedom's Children: Young Civil Rights Activists Tell Their Own Stories*, by Ellen Levine. Recently, I was encouraged that some efforts are being made to give credit to young civil rights activists when I saw Claudette included in Phillip Hoose's book, *We Were There, Too!* on young people in history and in Mary Turck's *The Civil Rights Movement for Kids: A History with Twenty-one Activities*. Our students learn about Rosa Parks, but they also need to hear about Claudette and other young people who were brave enough to take a stand and who played key roles in the civil rights movement.

Once the bus boycott began after Rosa Parks' arrest, hundreds of schoolchildren participated. For some, like thirteen-year-olds Joseph Lacey and Fred Taylor, this meant walking. "Everybody stuck together on the boycott," Joseph Lacey said. "It lasted over a year, and we walked. . . . Everybody felt like a part of the struggle . . ." (Levine 1993, 27).

Princella Howard reflected on her involvement. "The boycott . . . was so powerful. In a year you can build a great momentum. . . . I was eight and nine years old, but I understood clearly. Kids know when some people look down at you" (Levine 1993, 30).

In my search for children who were involved in the civil rights movement, I was so focused on children who lived in the areas where major events happened that it didn't occur to me that there might be children elsewhere who voiced their concern. Imagine my surprise and delight when I read about a letter written to President Eisenhower in 1956 by Franne Levine, a fifth grader. She wrote, "I don't think it is fair to make the Negroes sit in the back of busses down south. What if the Negroes made us sit in the back of busses and we had to work for them? I don't think we would like it" (Leotta and Haverkamp 1993, 42). (Although we say African Americans today, during this period the term *Negro* was used by most people, black and white, and is found in many quotes by leaders of the civil rights movement.) I found this when I read an article in *Cobblestone* about a National Archives exhibit celebrating our First Amendment right to petition (Leotta 1993). I wondered what other petitions were written by children—the article said there were many. This piece of information led me on another search.

A number of young people in the civil rights era are known in relation to the struggle to integrate schools. Many of us have heard of Ruby Bridges and Elizabeth Eckford. Some of our students may have seen the film about Ruby's integration of an elementary school in New Orleans in 1960, when she was six years old, or read the book she wrote for children, *Through My Eyes*. Ruby Bridges' book includes numerous photographs, some of Ruby's crayon drawings, and the recollections of her teacher for that year. Rather than face integration, all of the white parents withdrew their children from the school. Barbara Henry, Ruby's teacher, tells about her experience with her only pupil:

> I told her the other children would come back to school eventually. . . . Ruby never complained, but I knew she was lonely. Nowadays, when I'm invited into schools to

talk about that year, I find that Ruby's story so inspires children. They feel they finally have a hero who is like them. Ruby's story allows children to feel they, too, can do very important things and they, too, can be heroes. (Bridges 1999, 44)

Elizabeth Eckford was fifteen when she and eight others became the first black students at Central High School in Little Rock, Arkansas. They became known as the Little Rock Nine. The day-to-day insults and threats they faced made their year at the school almost unbearable, but they drew strength from each other and from the growing numbers of people who supported them. Elizabeth recalls:

> Thanks to a number of people, especially our parents, we never forgot the reasons we were attending Central High School. It was up to us to make integration a success, and if you think about it that way, then you realize that when you believe in something, even if you're afraid, you'll find a way to accomplish your goals. (Rochelle 1993, 21)

Sit-ins were used to protest segregation in places like movie theaters, libraries, and restaurants. Numerous young people who had been trained in Dr. Martin Luther King Jr.'s nonviolent methods, sat in these places and were arrested. In Levine's book, *Freedom's Children*, Frances Foster, James Roberson, Barbara Howard, and others give details about how they managed different sit-ins. Students who read their vivid descriptions would be able to picture themselves right there with protesters, sitting stoically at a lunch counter when a worker throws a bucket of water on them, or speaking politely but firmly when being insulted and arrested.

In Birmingham, Alabama, so many young people were arrested and injured in the marches that these demonstrations were labeled the Children's Crusade. In Phillip Hoose's *We Were There, Too!* students can read a firsthand account by Carolyn McKinstry, who was fourteen when she took part in one of these events in 1963. She tells about going to a meeting where Dr. King spoke to prepare participants for the protest, and about attending classes that trained children in nonviolence. She describes the power of the huge water hose that was turned on the marchers and how she tried to get away from it:

> When they finally turned it off I scooted around the side of the building and felt for my sweater. They had blasted a hole right through it. And then . . . I reached up and touched my hair. It was gone, on the right side of my head. My hair, gone. I was furious, and insulted. Why did they have to do that? (Hoose 2001, 222–223)

Sheyann Webb was eight when she became a civil rights activist. She was one of the youngest marchers on the day that became known as "Bloody Sunday" because hundreds of people in Selma were beaten. Sheyann is featured in Ellen

Levine's book *Freedom's Children* (1993). Teachers can also select portions from her book published with Rachel (West) Nelson, *Selma, Lord, Selma: Girlhood Memories of the Civil Rights Days*. Rachel, Sheyann's friend and neighbor, was nine at the time. They are pictured with Dr. King just before the march from Selma in the photograph in Figure 5–1. When they were in their late teens, they told Birmingham newspaperman Frank Sikora about what had happened to them. How they felt about their experiences, the fears they had, and how they handled those fears are expressed vividly in their book (Webb and Nelson 1980).

As your students read these interviews and recollections, they may wonder how these children found the courage to take such risks, and why they continued when their friends were injured or even killed, as four young girls were when their church was bombed on a Sunday morning in 1963. You might respond to their questions by reading to them what Bernita Roberson felt motivated her and gave her courage to continue.

> You would hear about everything that was going on, and you soon get it in your mind that you want to be a part of it. So every Monday night I went with my father (to the mass meetings). . . . Dr. King made the call for people to join him. . . . So I . . . volunteered. . . . We started out from Sixteenth Street Church. We held hands and just walked. Dr. King was leading. . . . They (the police) carried us to the county jail. All of us were in the same cell. . . . Then they started taking out the younger ones to . . . Juvenile. As we went out, Martin King was at the door of the cell because he was in jail also. He hugged us and shook all of our hands as we passed him. . . . I was determined to make a difference. I did not want to be intimidated by whites. (Levine 1993, 82–83)

Intimidation permeated the everyday lives of black children growing up with segregation. Leon Tillage tells about the oppression and hatred he saw and experienced growing up in North Carolina in his 1997 book *Leon's Story*. He walked to his school while white students, who had the privilege of riding buses to their school, called him names and threw things at him. When Leon was not in school, he helped his father, who was a sharecropper. He writes about frightening encounters with Klansmen, the beatings of African Americans who accidentally neglected to use the areas marked "colored," and his own later involvement in marches. When parents warned their children that they could get beaten or killed for marching, Leon and other youth would say, "We're getting beat up now. . . . So I'd rather get beat up for doing something . . . to change things. I mean, why get beat up for nothing?" (Tillage 1997, 88).

After reading or hearing accounts by those who were involved in the civil rights movement when they were young, our students can better empathize with them and their situations. The development of empathy is important in promoting

Figure 5–1. Sheyann Webb, left, and Rachel West with Martin Luther King Jr. on March 23, 1965, in Selma, Alabama, just before their march (Vernon Merritt/Black Star).

good prosocial or altruistic behavior in students. Laura Berk (1999) states that empathy is a predictor of prosocial behavior and refers to the research of Roberts and Strayer (1996) supporting this. As today's students learn more about the experiences of children their own age during the civil rights era, they are more likely to be motivated to themselves take a stand against prejudice and work for the fair treatment of all people. When teachers provide learning opportunities like these, we are helping our students become more empathetic.

Seeing segments of newscasts about actual events in which children were involved also helps our students empathize with the children; they cannot help but appreciate the courage and sacrifices those young people made. As they view the mobs' hateful faces and hear the insults hurled each day at those who integrated the schools, students can understand the risks that their earlier counterparts took. The PBS video *Fighting Back: 1957–1962*, part of the Eyes on the Prize series, begins by showing Ruby Bridges entering her new elementary school with a guard and continues by focusing on the Little Rock Nine integrating a high school. The first part of this video, up to the graduation of one of the high school students, could be shown to older students. Interviews with both black and white students give insights into their thoughts and feelings about integration. There is also a Disney movie on Ruby Bridges. It is not a primary source, but it might add to younger students' understanding of Ruby's struggle as she attended school by herself and coped with racism at so young an age.

Student Rights

Young people became involved in another issue in the 1960s. Imagine again: You are in a middle-school classroom where students are role-playing a court scene, improvising what they think might have been said. The chairs and desks have been arranged to simulate a court room. The student playing the judge is wearing a borrowed chorus robe. He bangs the gavel, calls the court to order, and asks the lawyer for the plaintiffs to call his first witness. A student takes the stand and the lawyer begins asking questions.

> PLAINTIFFS' LAWYER: Why did you wear a black armband with the peace symbol on it to school?
>
> STUDENT 1: I wore it to honor those who have already died in this war and to support Senator Robert Kennedy's suggestion that there be a truce.
>
> PLAINTIFFS' LAWYER: On what date did you first wear it?
>
> STUDENT 1: Friday, December 17, 1965. I was going to wear it on Thursday, but I heard the principals were against it. I felt we should try to talk to the school board first. The president of the board would not call an emergency meeting, so some of us wore them Friday.

PLAINTIFFS' LAWYER: What happened on Friday?

STUDENT 1: The principal asked me to take it off. When I didn't, he asked me to leave the school.

JUDGE: Will the lawyer for the school board question the witness?

DEFENDANT'S LAWYER: Since your parents are antiwar activists, didn't the idea of wearing armbands come from them?

STUDENT 1: No, some friends brought me a copy of a document saying that some students in Iowa were going to wear armbands.

DEFENDANT'S LAWYER: You knew about the rule against wearing armbands, yet you wore one to school anyway. Were there any disturbances at school when others saw it?

STUDENT 1: Some friends complimented me and others made bad remarks.

DEFENDANT'S LAWYER: So, you did create some disturbances by wearing the armband.

STUDENT 1: Well, not any more than usually occurs in school. I did hope others would ask me questions about why I was wearing it, because it's important to me that people are getting killed over there.

(Based on trial information in Rappaport 1993)

As the trial continues, two other young people are called for questioning. The judge rules in favor of the school board. The role-play continues with students pretending to be news reporters interviewing the plaintiffs' lawyer, who firmly states that he will take the case all the way to the Supreme Court if necessary.

Obviously, the issue is the Vietnam War and student rights are on trial. The case, *Tinker v. Des Moines*, may not be familiar to many of us. The three witnesses are John Tinker, fifteen, his sister Mary Beth, thirteen, and Chris Eckhardt, fifteen. The case did go to the Supreme Court, which ruled in favor of John, Mary Beth, and Chris. The decision was based on free speech and the application of the First Amendment to those in school. Your students might be interested in finding out how the stand taken by the three young people affects their own rights today. Doreen Rappaport edited legal documents from the trials for this case to re-create trials and hearings in her book *Tinker v. Des Moines*. She poses questions at different stages in her re-creation to give the readers opportunity to decide what they would do or say.

Women's Suffrage

During the women's suffrage movement, young girls took a stand for the rights of women. Among other activities, they joined their mothers in parades for the right to vote (Figure 5–2). In a *New York Times* article about an event on May 5, 1912, the reporter describes women of all ages, including young children and

Figure 5–2. Girls carrying a banner in a women's suffrage march (Getty Images).

schoolgirls, dressed in white and carrying banners. Teachers carried banners commenting about the problem of illiteracy under men's rule (Deitch 2000b, 25–28).

Lucy Haessler, who went to marches with her mother, described her experience:

> I was only ten years old the first time I went to a march with my mother. She told me, "Oh, you're too young. . . ." But I said, "I am going, because you're going to win the right to vote and I'm going to vote when I'm grown-up." So she let me march. . . . Just like the other suffragettes, I wore a white blouse and skirt, and a purple and gold sash that came across my front. Purple and gold were the colors of the women's suffrage movement. . . . I was so excited. (Colman 2000, 141)

In her midteens, Edna Purtell was a recognized leader of the movement. When the Connecticut legislature voted against suffrage in 1917, she started working for the National Women's Party. She participated in a women's suffrage march in Washington, D.C. When Edna and others were arrested, they went on a hunger strike. She was the youngest to do this (Hoose 2001, 181).

Some of the people who became leaders in the women's suffrage movement had strong feelings about discrimination against women when they were quite young. Elizabeth Cady Stanton was the daughter of a judge. When she was ten, she heard him counseling a woman whose drunken husband had mortgaged the farm she had inherited from her father. The judge explained that the law specified that a woman's property became her husband's when she married. The crying woman begged him to find something in his law books to help her. He took up a law book and read the Married Woman's Property Law to her. As the woman left, Elizabeth followed her and explained that she had a plan to help because she kept track of the pages in the law books that made her father's clients sad. She told the distraught woman, "I'm going to take my scissors and cut out every page that makes ladies cry" (from the Archives of the Seneca Falls Historical Society in Hodges 1998, Document 29a).

Martha Carey Thomas, who also became a leader of the movement and helped to found Bryn Mawr College, showed her strong feelings about women's suffrage in her diary in 1871, when she was fourteen. In reaction to hearing a lecture by Anna Dickinson, a brilliant orator on women's rights, Martha wrote, "Oh my, how terrible, how fearfully unjust. A girl certainly [should] do what she chooses as well as a boy. When I grow up—we'll see what will happen" (Thomas 1979, 48 in Hoobler and Hoobler 1999, 101).

Children and young people helped make the civil rights movement a success, and some were involved in the women's suffrage movement, too. When I read their accounts, I wondered how many of today's students might feel strongly about injustices in the world now, and how their feelings might be the beginning of a lifetime of concern about the fair and equal treatment of all people.

Using the Resources

Participating in Dramatic Activities

Enacting the bus scene and trial scene simulations described in this chapter enabled the students to experience some of the emotions involved in the historical events and helped them understand the feelings and actions of children who worked for civil rights and students' rights in the 1950s and 1960s. According to Joyce and Weil (1996), role-playing and simulation foster the development of empathy and problem-solving and decision-making skills. Teachers who use drama in the classroom say that their students have an increased tolerance of people's differences, better motivation, and critical-thinking skills. In addition, using various forms of improvisation gives students the opportunity to contribute to their own learning (Frieberg and Driscoll 1996).

I have found Shaftel and Shaftel's (1982) book *Role Playing in the Curriculum* to be very helpful in designing role-plays. According to these authors, students can relive incidents through role-playing, then investigate what happened and discuss what the results would have been if other choices had been made in the situation. To enable students to do dramatic activities, I follow the steps that Shaftel and Shaftel give, adding my own variations as needed.

1. Warming up the group by confronting the problem.
2. Selecting the role-players who will participate in the dramatization.
3. Preparing the rest of the class to participate as observers.
4. Setting the stage.
5. Enacting the scene.
6. Discussing and evaluating the role-play.
7. Expanding on the enactment by replaying it with revised roles, playing suggested next steps, or exploring alternative possibilities.
8. Sharing experiences and generalizing.

For example, for Step 1, if the students were going to role-play a sit-in at a luncheonette during the civil rights movement, I might present the sit-in described by fourteen-year-old Frances Foster in Levine's *Freedom's Children*. I would begin by telling my students who she was and that it was her first demonstration. Frances and her friend went to a store, purchased some books, and then sat down at the luncheonette on the mezzanine. A young black waitress was afraid to come to their table and wait on them; maybe she thought she would lose her job or cause something bad to happen to the girls. A white woman told them that they knew they couldn't eat there. Frances and her friend told her that they had purchased some books and their money was accepted by the store; now they wanted to order some food. A white man came up and told them to leave. He pointed to the policeman standing outside and said that he would ask the policeman to remove the girls if they didn't leave. At this point in the story, I would stop and ask my students to talk about what the issues were and what they think the girls might do.

In Step 2, the students would list the roles to be played and decide who would play them. To prepare the observers (all students not playing a role), I would tell them to be prepared to describe the role-players' expressions and feelings, to think of what consequences the action portrayed might have had, and to consider alternatives to the action. To set the stage (Step 4), we would place several tables with a few chairs around them at the front of the classroom.

Following this first role-play (Step 5), the actors would express how they felt playing the roles and the observers would talk about their reactions to the choices made by the two girls, other actions that could be taken, the possible consequences of the actions, and what feelings and emotions the role-players showed (Step 6). Then those who had role-played would become observers and other students would enact a second role-play (Step 7). The class would then discuss and

116

evaluate the second enactment. Finally, I'd have all students describe their ideas and feelings about the entire experience and make generalizations about what impact repeated sit-ins might have had on the civil rights movement.

Many of the accounts of children involved in the civil rights movement could be developed into role-plays or other dramatic activities. To represent children's participation in marches, students could learn some of the songs they sang, such as "Oh, Freedom" and "We Shall Overcome," and march while they sing. In relation to women's suffrage, Elizabeth Cady Stanton's childhood concern about the Women's Property Law and Lucy Haessler's confrontation with her mother about marching would make good skits. Students could also pretend to be participants in a women's suffrage parade by making banners and marching for the right to vote.

Studying Videos and Photographs

The PBS video series *Eyes on the Prize* is based on archival footage and interviews of people in the civil rights movement. In a study on the impact of this series, Brier and Kinsler reported that teachers thought it was the best video history series they had ever used (Richardson 1992). To prepare your students for viewing the segment on school integration, first introduce the students who integrated the schools. This can be done by reading or having your students read Ruby Bridges' book and the recollections of the Little Rock Nine. Elizabeth Eckford, who is shown arriving at the school by herself in Figure 5–3, and Ernest Green, who was the first to graduate, could be presented in more depth. Learning about these young people will set the context for your students to watch the video segment, which should conclude with Green's graduation. It is important that you emphasize that what the students will see is actual footage, not actors playing roles:

> Students have become so accustomed to seeing recreations of events, simulated violence, and artificial drama and emotionality that they need to be reminded that what they are about to witness is a piece of history, not a piece of fiction. (Lavelle 1992, 346)

Next, give your students some guidance about what to observe when they watch the video. Here are some things that you might suggest:

1. Look at the faces of the nine students and the emotions they portray. Try to imagine what these young people were thinking and feeling.
2. Look at the faces of the people protesting desegregation. What emotions do you see reflected there?
3. Imagine yourself walking with Elizabeth Eckford as she attempts to go to school. What do you feel and experience?

4. A reporter questions two white girls about what they feel is the cause of the conflict about integrating the school. How do they respond? What do they think about the situation?

5. As you view the segment, jot down what you observe and feel.

You may need to show the video segment a second time to allow your students to form more in-depth impressions. One experienced educator suggests that teachers use the pause button on the remote control at various points when viewing the documentary, pausing to really look at a scene, to ask a question, or to

Figure 5–3. Elizabeth Eckford, age fifteen, attempting to enter Central High School in Little Rock, Arkansas, in 1957 (Bettmann/Corbis).

explain something if students seem confused (Lavelle 1992). This helps them interpret and actively explore what they are viewing. Discuss the five suggestions above after the viewing.

Similar questions focused on feelings and reactions could be used to guide studies of photographs. For example, if you use the photograph of Elizabeth Eckford walking to school, you might ask the following:

1. What do you imagine Elizabeth is feeling? Thinking? Why?
2. What do you imagine the crowd is feeling? Thinking? Why?
3. If you were in the scene, what would you say to Elizabeth? To the crowd? Why?

Questions about the photograph of Sheyann Webb and Rachel West with Dr. King (Figure 5–1) might include these:

1. Look closely at Sheyann's and Rachel's faces. If they could talk to you, what might they say?
2. What would you ask them at this time just before they march?

For photographs of girls in a women's suffrage march, students could discuss these questions:

1. What do the faces of the girls at the front show you about what they are thinking and how they are feeling? Why?
2. What do you think the people on the sidewalk are thinking about what they see? Why?
3. Why do you think these girls are participating in this parade?
4. What in the photograph tells you this was taken in the early 1900s?

Experiencing Guided Imagery

Guided imagery is an effective strategy to help students imagine what children in other time periods experienced. I have used this method to introduce students to Ruby Bridges, basing my guided imagery on Ruby's autobiography, *Through My Eyes*. I relate her experiences using the pronouns "you" and "your" and speaking in present tense to give a "you are there" feeling. I begin by saying something like the following:

> It's Sunday night. Your mother tells you that you're going to a different school tomorrow. She says there will be a lot of people around the school, but she will be with you. You feel sad because you will miss your friends at your old school. Now it's Monday morning and four white men come to drive you and your mother to school. You find out they are U.S. federal marshals. Now you are at William Frantz School.

There are people shouting and police everywhere. You think it may be Mardi Gras, since that is a noisy time in New Orleans. The four men surround you and your mother and go with you inside. As you sit in the principal's office all day, you see white parents taking their children out of your new school.

To prepare students for this guided imagery, I ask them to close their eyes and relax as we take a trip back in time. I count backwards: 2003, 2002, 2001, 2000, 1990, 1980, 1970, 1960. I tell them to imagine that they are six years old and living in New Orleans. With their eyes still closed, I take them through the imagery, beginning with the passage above and continuing with more of Ruby's experiences. Then I ask my students to open their eyes and either draw or express in writing what they felt as they experienced the imagery. After this, the students share their responses with the class. This way of creating guided imagery can be used with the recollections of Elizabeth Eckford, Sheyann Webb, and others who were active in the civil rights movement when they were young.

Connecting Events with Students' Experiences

Relating the experiences of children who were involved in the civil rights and women's suffrage movements to our students' own experiences is another effective way to enable students to identify with children in history. For example, before introducing Ruby Bridges, Elizabeth Eckford, or any of the others to your class, you could ask your students to share their experiences of and feelings about going to a new school. Did they feel accepted? Was it hard to make friends? Suppose there were people who did not want them in the school—how would they feel? What would they do? For the introduction to his third-grade lesson plan on Ruby Bridges, Angelo Ciardiello suggests asking a class if they have ever been in a situation where they felt alone and scared (2001). Before they meet Claudette Colvin, have the class imagine that there is a law that everyone between the ages of six and fifteen always has to sit at the back of buses, planes, or train cars, even if they are traveling with older members of their families who sit separately. What would their reaction be? In relation to those involved in sit-ins, ask your students to imagine not being allowed to go to a favorite restaurant or sit where they want in a movie theater. To connect them with children who marched for civil rights or women's suffrage, ask your students if any of them have been in a parade or participated in a march. Would they march if they knew people would yell at them or try to stop them? Ask your students if they have ever been discriminated against or treated unfairly. Questions like these help our students understand the frustrations earlier children faced and the courage they needed to take action. Teachers know that a general principle of learning is that "students learn more effectively when they relate new information to the things they already know" (Ormrod

2003, 15). This principle supports taking the time to ask our students to make connections between their own lives and the lives of historical children.

Engaging in Researching, Writing, and Making Comparisons

As your students begin to identify and empathize with young activists, they will be motivated to find out more about them and their periods of history. For an overview of the civil rights movement, they could take an interactive tour at the National Civil Rights Museum website (*www.civilrightsmuseum.org*), which would help them understand how the events fit together chronologically. Searching under the topics "Votes for Women" or "Civil Rights" at the Library of Congress's American Memory site (*www.memory.loc.gov*) would lead them to further information. There is a website that displays 1957 front pages from the *Arkansas Democrat* and *Arkansas Gazette* covering the integration of Central High School in Little Rock. This site, *www.ardemgaz.com/prev/central*, includes photographs of the nine young people and the angry mobs they encountered. The website for the Ruby Bridges Foundation, *www.rubybridges.org*, might also be of interest. It has pictures that news reporters took, articles, Ruby's story, and information on how you can invite Ruby to your school. Students can also use the resources listed at the end of this book for even more in-depth exploration.

As part of this investigation, students could be given questions for inquiry. Possibilities include the following:

- What motivated these children and young people to participate?
- How did they find the courage to face the challenges and dangers of becoming involved?
- How were they trained and prepared for participating?
- What was the most challenging situation each one faced? Why?

It is important that students also be encouraged to develop their own questions, which makes their inquiry process more meaningful and authentic. The suggestions for conducting inquiry studies in Chapter 2 can be used to guide your students in selecting or creating questions, developing hypotheses, finding information, and drawing conclusions.

Once your students really get familiar with the children of the civil rights movement, they will have the knowledge base to engage in creative and critical-thinking activities. They might choose one of the young activists, such as Sheyann Webb or Elizabeth Eckford, and write a letter asking that person something they wish to know about her and describing their own feelings about what the person did. It would be interesting to have your students exchange their letters and have each one answer pretending to be the activist to whom the letter is addressed.

Some students might pretend to be reporters for a paper or magazine and write imaginary interviews with children involved in the civil rights movement. It would provide an interesting contrast to create an "interview" of one of the white people in the mobs. For example, in the photograph of Elizabeth Eckford in Figure 5–3, there is an angry girl in a white dress at Elizabeth's right who is yelling at her. Students could write a letter to this girl or pretend to interview her. Perhaps they could try to persuade her to think differently and change her feelings about integration. If they do write to this girl, tell them that five years after this photograph was taken, the girl was so ashamed that she called Elizabeth and said she was sorry about what she had done (Hoose 2001, 219). Activities like these help students to "compare ways in which people from different cultures think about and deal with their . . . social conditions" and "explain why individuals and groups respond differently to their . . . social environments and/or changes to them on the basis of shared assumptions, values, and beliefs" (NCSS 1994, 33).

Processes that give students opportunities for critical thinking, such as comparing and analyzing, can be used with primary and secondary sources by and about the children in the civil rights movement. This helps students think more deeply and in a more meaningful way (Eggen 2001, 344). In addition, it helps them meet one of the NCSS "Time, Continuity, and Change" standards to "compare and contrast different . . . accounts about past events, people, places, or situations" (34). Your students could compare primary sources in which Claudette Colvin, Elizabeth Eckford, Ruby Bridges, Sheyann Webb, and others describe their own experiences with secondary sources describing the same people and events. For example, Chapter 9 in Belinda Rochelle's (1993) *Witnesses to Freedom*, about Sheyann Webb, could be compared with Sheyann's own lengthy recollection in *Freedom's Children*. Robert Coles' book *The Story of Ruby Bridges* (1995) might be compared with *Through My Eyes*, Ruby Bridges' autobiography. Using a graphic organizer like a Venn diagram, ask your students to list what type of information is found in each resource that is not in the other, and what information is found in both sources. Which type of source helps them feel more connected to the person? What are the advantages and disadvantages of each type?

In the same way, photographs can be compared with illustrations created by artists. As an example, if students compare photographs of Ruby Bridges with George Ford's illustrations in *The Story of Ruby Bridges*, ask what feelings come to them and what can they learn about Ruby as they view each one. What is different and similar about the photos and illustrations? Some of the drawings Ruby made during her first year of school integration could also be analyzed to see what they express about her experience. These drawings can be found in *Through My Eyes* and in Coles' book *Their Eyes Meeting the World: Listening to Children: The Drawings and Paintings of Children* (1995). To facilitate analysis, ask your students questions such as the following: What do you see in the drawing? How do you think she was feeling when she drew the picture? What in the drawings shows that she felt alone? (Ruby's drawing of her school in *Through My Eyes* shows no children, for example.)

Conducting Interviews

The civil rights movement is recent enough for students to be able to locate and interview adults who were young during that time. Actual interviews can serve as models for doing this. A powerful one to use in this way is Charlayne Hunter Gault's interview of Ruby Bridges Hall on February 18, 1997, for the PBS News Hour. Students can listen to it or read the transcript on the PBS website (*www.pbs.org/newshour/bb/*). They can then evaluate the interview, suggest other questions, and talk about what they learned about Ruby from the interview. For example, how did Ruby feel about not being prepared by her parents for what was happening? Why did she pray for the people in the mob who were so angry at her? Discussing what they discovered from this interview will help your students frame questions to ask in the interviews they will conduct.

Interviews that children have conducted with adults who were young during the civil rights movement are excellent models. *Oh, Freedom! Kids Talk about the Civil Rights Movement with the People Who Made It Happen* (King and Osborne 1997) is an interesting collection of interviews. In the book, Matthew Jackson interviews his mother about her marches and sit-ins in Kansas. Ruth Welter talks with Bernice Johnson about how she sang "Oh, Freedom" as she marched for justice in Georgia. Students would find it interesting to read some of these and find examples of how follow-up questions can be used to probe for more information in an interview.

To locate adults who were children during the civil rights era, your students could invite their families, community members, local organizations, and the school staff to help in their search. Once located, you could select suitable interviewees and invite them to your classroom to be interviewed. These adults may or may not have been actively involved in the movement. If they were, your students can ask what they did, why they participated, and how they felt about their involvement. If they were not, the students can ask what they recall about the time and what their impressions were. Suggestions for preparing children to conduct interviews are given in Chapter 2.

I tend to think of the benefits of interviewing from the perspective of students and the knowledge and skills they gain from the experience. However, I discovered a benefit to those being interviewed when I read about a wonderful result of two interviews conducted by sixteen-year-old students in Kansas. In 1996, Heather Jurgensen decided to interview Elizabeth Eckford for her National

History Day project when she discovered that Eckford was still living in Little Rock. Eckford told Heather about Ken Reinhardt Jr., a white student who always spoke to her and treated her as if she were any other student. Because he did this, he was threatened and roughed up by some of the other students. When two of Jurgensen's classmates found out about Reinhardt, they interviewed him. Reinhardt, who was a banker in Louisville, Kentucky, decided to fly to Little Rock for a reunion with Eckford (Yamasaki 1998).

A strong rationale for using the variety of activities suggested in this section is Howard Gardner's theory of multiple intelligences (1983). Our students' diverse abilities are supported and developed when we use a variety of teaching methods. Role-play, guided imagery, film, interviews, drawing, writing, research, and analyzing photographs and art support students' special interests and talents. For example, role-playing and interviewing involve linguistic and interpersonal intelligences. Participating in guided imagery, viewing videos and photographs, and drawing involve spatial intelligence. Using either the visual or performing arts can be especially meaningful. "What all of the arts have in common is their capacity to generate emotion, to stimulate and to express the 'feel' for a situation, individual, or object" (Eisner 2002, 554). This helps students "develop critical sensitivities such as empathy and skepticism regarding attitudes, values, and behaviors of people," which is one of the NCSS standards under the theme "Time, Continuity, and Change" (NCSS 1994, 34).

Young Activists Today

Our students can be empowered to work against discrimination and for justice, fairness, and the equal treatment of all people. Not only do they have the examples of the historical children presented in this chapter to empower them, they can be inspired by what other children and young people are doing today. Ryan White's battle in the late 1980s against the discrimination children with AIDS faced is well known, although today's students may not be familiar with his inspiring story. When he was barred from school, he sued for the right to attend school. Ryan and his family were harassed both before and after the court ruled that his school had to let him return. Many parents kept their children home when he returned to school. After moving to another town, Ryan traveled to schools and even wrote a book to help children understand HIV and AIDS. Ryan felt that if he could help children understand AIDS, they could help change their parents' attitudes. When he died in 1990, he had influenced millions (Cunningham 1993).

In South Africa, a little more than a decade after Ryan's death, twelve-year-old Nkosi Johnson died after his struggle with the disease. His heroic efforts in speaking against discrimination and for government action to keep AIDS from spreading were praised around the world in newspapers and on TV. Whenever I tell students and other teachers about Nkosi and show them the photograph in Figure 5–4, taken of him speaking at an international AIDS conference, they are moved at seeing this frail twelve-year-old speaking in front of a large audience. A *New York Times* article quotes Nkosi as saying, "Care for us and accept us. . . . Don't be afraid of us—we are all the same!" (McNeil 2001, A3).

Teachers can involve students in looking through newspapers and magazines for articles on children and young people who are taking action to bring about the just and fair treatment of people and to combat prejudice and discrimination. They might also take notes on any such children they happen to see on television. The articles they find and notes they take can be shared in class, incorporated into a bulletin board display, or placed in plastic sleeves in a three-ring binder as a class library reference.

Although their stories are not as well known as Nkosi Johnson's and Ryan White's, other children's actions are recorded in juvenile literature. In *It's Our World, Too!*, Phillip Hoose includes the stories of two young people who wouldn't accept discrimination and a third who overcame her hesitation at being with people who had Alzheimer's disease. Neto Villareal took action to get his high school to stop football fans from screaming racial insults at Hispanic American players. Sarah Rosen, a sixth-grade student, organized a march to protest what she viewed as discrimination against girls. Beni Seballos discovered through volunteering at a senior center that she had something in common with the people there and enjoyed helping them. Neto's concluding statement reflects the feeling of success all three felt. Neto and the other participating students at his school knew that they hadn't extinguished racial prejudice in their town, but "at least we made it known that we wouldn't accept racism in our school or from our fans. We made a difference in the part of our lives that we really could control" (Hoose 1993, 25).

Girls write about problems they discovered and the actions they took to help solve them in *Girls and Young Women Leading the Way: Twenty True Stories About Leadership* by Frances Karnes and Suzanne Bean. An interesting problem involving equal rights was solved by fifth-graders Lee Palmer and Janine Givens. Their library in Andover, Massachusetts, did not allow children under grade seven to use the main floor on their own. Since this floor housed young adult collections as well as the biography and magazine sections, the girls believed that the policy was unfair. They wrote a petition, contacted the American Civil Liberties Union, and even appeared on Boston radio and TV stations until they succeeded in changing the policy. Through this experience they gained confidence to continue to take a stand against other things they believe to be wrong (Karnes and Bean 1993).

Through reading about the processes that young activists use to bring about change and what they have to say about their experiences, our students will

Figure 5–4. Nkosi Johnson from Johannesburg, South Africa, speaking at the Thirteenth International AIDS conference (AP/Wide World Photos).

develop ideas about how to solve the problems and issues that are of concern to them. What can our students do? They might begin with their own school: Are there any inequities? Is everyone being treated fairly and with respect?

After September 11, 2001, many Arab Americans encountered discrimination. I recently read a newspaper article about a Muslim family who decided to move because the children were being harassed in school. However, incidents occurred in their new location, too. The father stated that the school system had been supportive: "From the tone I heard, they don't tolerate this" (Mulvaney 2003, B6).

Students can brainstorm ways to promote equal treatment and to do something about problem situations. There are excellent ideas for things students can do in the Anti-Defamation League's book *Hate Hurts: How Children Learn and Unlearn Prejudice* (Stern-LaRosa and Bettmann 2000). Some of the more interesting activities include creating skits that promote diversity, writing and performing a song celebrating their school's diversity, thinking of antiprejudice slogans to print as bumper stickers, and creating a pledge against prejudice to recite in classrooms and at school assemblies.

Your students might be interested in planning and carrying out one of the ideas suggested in *Girls and Young Women Leading the Way*. Two that I especially like are planning a game or puppet show for younger children on how people of all races can get along, and interviewing people of all ages and races in their community and school to discover their ideas about how to improve race relations. A follow-up to the latter project is to share the ideas obtained from the interviews with others in the school and to actually begin implementing some of them.

The inspiring actions of children in the past and today will encourage our students to work for the equal and fair treatment of other people. Statements of children near their age can give them the confidence to believe, as did Lee Palmer and Janine Givens, that "kids can change things with help and guidance from adults. . . . If you believe in something strong enough, there are no limits to what you can do, even if you're a kid . . ." (Karnes and Bean 1993, 38).

6

Discovering Children in Other Times and Places

In 1922, in the Valley of the Kings in Egypt, Howard Carter, an English archaeologist unearths stairs leading down to a secret door to a pharaoh's tomb. He reads the name on the door: TUTANKHAMEN! He enters chambers filled with treasures and items that the king enjoyed or needed when he was alive. He finally comes to the golden coffin and raises the lid. He removes a beautiful gold mask and looks at the face. He sees— a young man!

King Tut became pharaoh in the mid-1300s B.C. when he was nine and died when he was only eighteen. Students learning about ancient Egypt can discover what his life was like by looking at pictures of the objects found in his tomb and reading descriptions of them. For example, bows and arrows tell us that Tut liked to hunt and four *senet* boards indicate that he must have liked games, particularly senet, which is something like checkers. Students who read Robert Sabuda's 1994 book *Tutankhamen's Gift* will find out that more temples and monuments were built during this young king's short reign than in the reign of any other pharaoh.

We can introduce our students to specific historical children who lived long ago when we teach about earlier periods of history. In this chapter, we meet some of those earlier children, as well as more recent ones who didn't seem to fit into the themes of the other chapters. Ways that we and our students can continue discovering information about the children who lived in whatever time period we're studying will also be explored. This can become an ongoing and meaningful process for us and for our students.

Children Who Were Rulers and Princesses

Fiona Macdonald's wonderful 1998 book *A Child's Eye View of History: Discover History Through the Experiences of Children from the Past* has primary sources and beautiful, detailed illustrations, as well as photographs of artifacts. The stories of real children from ancient to modern times are told from contemporary evidence and through interviews, diaries, and letters. Through reading this book, your students can learn about other royal children, such as Lord Pacal, who in A.D. 615 at age twelve became king of a Mayan city-state, or Aiyaruk, a Mongol princess, who in about 1280 refused an arranged marriage and became a warrior.

Pocahontas is a princess who is probably familiar to many of our students. Numerous books have been written about this daughter of the chief of the Powhatan nation. She was twelve in 1607 when her tribe captured John Smith when he had left Jamestown to explore the James River. Most of what we know about her comes from Smith's writings. He describes how Pocahontas saved his life when her father ordered his execution. She became friendly with the British and must have felt torn about living in two worlds when more animosity developed between her father and the British. Eventually, she married John Rolfe, went to London, and died there when she was only twenty-two. In a letter to Queen Anne of England in 1616, John Smith wrote, "Had it not been for Pocahontas, Virginia might lie to this day as it was on our first arrival" (Hoose 2001, 14).

More than two centuries later, another young princess came under the protection of Queen Victoria and lived in what seemed to be two different worlds. As I write about this girl, she stares out at me from the cover of Walter Dean Myers' book *At Her Majesty's Request: An African Princess in Victorian England*, looking as if she wants to tell me more about her struggles as well as her experiences with royalty (Figure 6–1). She was born into a royal family in a West African village in 1843, and at age five was captured by Dahomian raiders. When she was seven, she was about to be sacrificed in a Dahomian tribal ritual but was rescued by a British officer, Commander Forbes. Forbes gave her the name Sarah Forbes Bonetta. She was taken to England on his ship, the *Bonetta*, and introduced to Queen Victoria, who took responsibility for Sarah even though she lived with the officer's family. Quotes from Queen Victoria's diary show her enjoyment of her visits with Sarah and her interest in the girl's care. Sarah lived a life of remarkable privilege in England because of her connection with the queen, but she also experienced a life of losses—her family and home in West Africa, and the family she became part of in England. In the conclusion to his biography, Myers attempts to summarize Sarah's life:

> She lost so many chances for fulfillment, and yet received so many different opportunities. . . . But was destined to be apart from the world in which she lived. Throughout all of her turmoil and triumphs, she . . . remained, always, a princess. (Myers 1999, 140)

Figure 6–1. Thirteen-year-old Sarah Forbes Bonetta in 1856 (The Royal Archives © Her Majesty Queen Elizabeth II/William Bambridge).

Children of U.S. Presidents

The children of U.S. presidents experience being in a very different world during the time they live in the White House. Students learning about Washington, D.C., or U.S. presidents might be curious about what young people who lived in the White House experienced and how they made the transition from one world to the other. Some children liked being in the limelight sometimes, but at other times wished for a more normal life. Some felt a certain loneliness when their fathers became presidents and they didn't have as much in common with their friends anymore. *Growing Up in the White House,* by Seymour Reit, and *First Chil-*

dren, by Katherine Leiner, describe the special experiences and numerous antics of presidents' children, as well as their complaints that "it is like living in a fish-bowl where everyone watches your every move and then talks about you in the newspapers and at private parties as if they knew you" (Leiner 1996, x). The antics of some of these children are amusing. Quentin and Archie, the children of Theodore Roosevelt, became known for their escapades. For example, when Archie was sick in bed with the measles, his brother Quentin managed to smuggle their pony, Algonquin, into Archie's bedroom.

Children Going on Adventures

When we study explorers, we rarely hear about the boys serving on ships who helped make their voyages possible. One of these is twelve-year-old Diego Bermudez, who signed to go on the *Santa Maria* with Columbus. He and even younger boys served as pages. Older boys were apprentice seamen. Boys from wealthy families were hired to be officers' personal servants. Phillip Hoose's *We Were There, Too!* lists the names of seventeen boys who sailed with Columbus. On his last voyage, Columbus took his son Ferdinand, who was thirteen.

In 1608 another young adventurer, thirteen-year-old Thomas Savage, sailed to Jamestown with the second group of English settlers. When John Smith found out that the Powhatan tribes exchanged children so that they could learn from each other, he decided to exchange Thomas with a boy of the Powhatan tribe. Thomas agreed to learn all that he could and to try to serve as a spy. After three years he returned to the Jamestown colony, where he was made an ensign and declared the interpreter for the colonies because of his knowledge of the Algo-nquian language.

The whaling industry attracted some young adventurers. Some boys, like George Fred Tilton (Figure 6–2), smuggled themselves aboard whalers. Phillip Hoose tells Tilton's story in *We Were There, Too!* George was fourteen when he slipped aboard the *Union*, anchored at New Bedford, Massachusetts. It is obvious that he had no idea what it would be like for he wrote of his first time in a rowboat pursuing a whale, then being towed by it after the whale was harpooned:

> Three days out of Bermuda we raised a sperm whale, and I was the most excited and anxious boy in the world. I wanted to lower and get him and I don't suppose that anyone moved any faster than I did when we got the order to lower. We went on to him and got fast without any fuss, but believe me, from that time on nobody wanted to get away from him any worse than I did. He made only sixty-five barrels, so you see he was a lot smaller than a great many whales that have been taken, but I was scared blue. . . . We cut him in, tried him out and stowed the oil below, but I hadn't got over my scare enough to learn how it was done. (Tilton 1928, 18)

131

Figure 6–2. Fourteen-year-old George Fred Tilton, 1870s (courtesy of Martha's Vineyard Historical Society).

George later became a ship captain and wrote a book about his life in the whaling industry, *Cap'n George Fred*.

Daniel Weston Hall was another fourteen-year-old who went to sea in a whaling ship. Diane Stanley tells Hall's story in her picture book *The True Adventures of Daniel Hall* (1995). Other children went on whaling ships because their fathers were captains. Laura Jernegan kept a diary as she traveled on whaling voyages. Her photograph and a copy of two pages from her diary are in Figures 6–3 and 6–4. Laura began her diary in 1868 at age six and continued it until she was nine. Here are two entries:

> Friday 5 (February 1869): It is a pleasant day and a fair wind. Papa saw diamond fish from the mast head. Prescott is out on deck.
>
> Wednesday 10: Papa has got two whales. Papa said that the men would boil out the bluber. There was a bird flew on board of the ship Roman. (Jernegan 2000, 14)

(When possible, show your students copies of pages from an original diary in addition to typed transcripts, even if part of the pages are not clear. When they see only transcripts, some students have trouble believing that they're actually reading the historical child's own words.)

A Whaling Captain's Daughter: The Diary of Laura Jernegan, 1868–1871 (2000) is one of the books in the Diaries, Letters, and Memoirs series published by Blue Earth Books. This book includes information about the whaling industry, photographs of children aboard whaling ships, and a time line, as well as lists of other related books, places to write and visit, and Internet sites.

These two sources about George Fred and Laura can help students understand the whaling industry from the perspectives of children. *Meet the Allens in Whaling Days* (Loeper 1999), a biographical story of a Nantucket whaling family, complements these sources and provides further background.

In 1909, sixteen-year-old Hermine Jahns traveled cross-country in a Maxwell automobile driven by twenty-one-year old Alice Ramsey, the first such trip made by a woman driver. Patricia Hyatt wrote a book in the form of a fictional diary of Hermine. Her *Coast to Coast with Alice* (1995) is based on newspaper stories, interviews, and Alice Ramsey's own memoir, *Veil, Duster, and Tire Iron*. Although we do not have any actual writing by Hermine, Hyatt's book includes photographs of her on the trip.

Children Helping Others

Sacagawea is another young person familiar to many of our students. Without the help of this Shoshone girl and other native people, Lewis and Clark would not

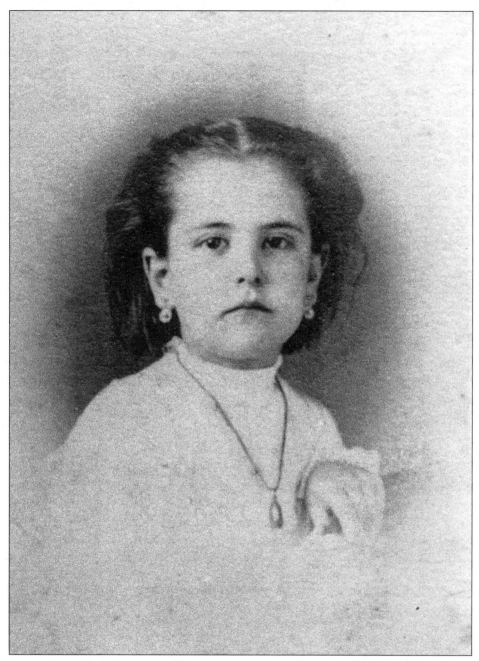

Figure 6–3. When she was six, Laura Jernegan began keeping a diary about living on a whaling ship (Martha's Vineyard Historical Society).

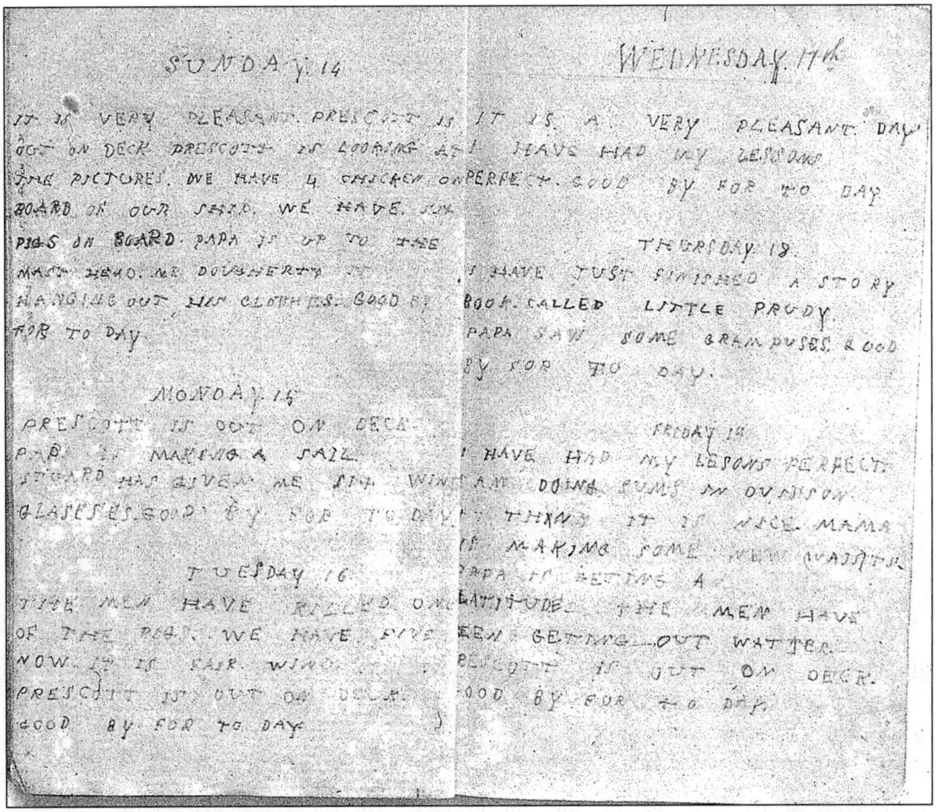

SUNDAY 14

IT IS VERY PLEASANT. PRESCOTT IS OUT ON DECK. PRESCOTT IS LOOKING AT THE PICTURES. WE HAVE 4 CHICKEN ON BOARD OF OUR SHIP. WE HAVE SIX PIGS ON BOARD. PAPA IS UP TO THE MAST HEAD. MR DOUGHERTY IS HANGING OUT HIS CLOTHES. GOOD BY FOR TO DAY

MONDAY 15

PRESCOTT IS OUT ON DECK. PAPA IS MAKING A SAIL. STEWARD HAS GIVEN ME SIX WINE GLASSES. GOOD BY FOR TO DAY

TUESDAY 16

THE MEN HAVE KILLED ONE OF THE PIGS. WE HAVE FIVE NOW. IT IS FAIR WIND. PRESCOTT IS OUT ON DECK. GOOD BY FOR TO DAY

WEDNESDAY 17th

IT IS A VERY PLEASANT DAY. I HAVE HAD MY LESSONS PERFECT. GOOD BY FOR TO DAY

THURSDAY 18.

I HAVE JUST FINISHED A STORY BOOK CALLED LITTLE PRUDY. PAPA SAW SOME GRAMPUSES. GOOD BY FOR TO DAY.

FRIDAY 19

I HAVE HAD MY LESONS PERFECT. I AM DOING SUMS IN DIVISION. I THINK IT IS NICE. MAMA IS MAKING SOME NEW CURTAINS. PAPA IS GETTING A LATITUDE. THE MEN HAVE BEEN GETTING OUT WATTER. PRESCOTT IS OUT ON DECK. GOOD BY FOR TO DAY.

Figure 6–4. Two pages from Laura Jernegan's diary written aboard her father's whaling ship (Martha's Vineyard Historical Society).

have reached the Pacific. Sacagawea was only fifteen when she became their guide in 1804. She also found sources of food for them and served as their interpreter with other tribes. In their journals, Lewis and Clark recorded the many ways Sacagawea helped during their expedition. Lewis wrote about her bravery in retrieving valuable articles that spilled from their boat during a sudden squall:

> The Indian woman to whom I ascribe equal fortitude and resolution with any person on board at the time of the accedent (accident) caught and preserved most of the light articles which were washed overboard. (DeVoto 1953, 111)

Older students can look through *The Journals of Lewis and Clark* (DeVoto) to find other passages about Sacagawea, such as an entry by Lewis describing how she searched through small piles of driftwood to locate wild artichokes mice had collected.

In *We Were There, Too!* Phillip Hoose has an excellent section on Sacagawea. A number of books about Sacagawea are available including David Adler's *A Picture book of Sacagawea* and Joseph Bruchac's *Sacagawea*. Bruchac includes excerpts from Lewis and Clark's journal in his book.

Louis Braille, who became blind when he was three years old, was determined to find a better way of creating books for people who were blind. In 1824, when he was fifteen, he figured out what would become the braille system. Russell Freedman's biography *Out of Darkness: The Story of Louis Braille* (1997) vividly describes Braille's life and how he created the system that has made reading possible for those who are blind.

Sacagawea and Louis Braille are just two of the young people featured in Dennis Fradin's *Remarkable Children: Twenty Who Made History*. This book is a good resource for teachers because it includes children from different time periods and countries.

Abbie Burgess and Kate Shelley were two young girls who showed courage and determination in the face of danger. Their stories, told in Margaret Wetterer's *Kate Shelley and the Midnight Express* and Peter and Connie Roop's *Keep the Lights Burning Abbie*, would appeal to younger readers. Abbie and her family lived in a lighthouse in Maine. In 1856, when her father was away and a tremendous storm came, she managed to keep the lighthouse lamps lit by herself during the entire week of the storm. Fifteen-year-old Kate Shelley's act of bravery in 1881 also involved a storm. She lived in Moingona, Iowa, near a creek. The water rose and the train bridge broke as an engine went over it. In spite of the flood, Kate was able to get to the train station to tell railroad workers there to stop the next train. Then she led them to the site of the crash where they rescued some survivors. Newspapers reported Kate's bravery to the entire nation. She received a gold medal from the state of Iowa and the railroad gave her a lifetime pass.

Children Writing Journals and Diaries in the 1800s

When I led a workshop on children in history at the Northeast Regional Conference for the Social Studies in Boston in 2003, the participants and I discussed the availability of children's diaries. A middle school teacher mentioned that he had used some girls' diaries with his classes. His male students, who had been intensely interested when he had used letters written by young soldiers in previous lessons, wanted to know why he didn't have any diaries written by boys. This teacher thought that perhaps writing diaries was something that girls tended to do more than boys. We discussed this, and shared resources written by boys. Several weeks later, I was delighted to locate the diary of an early American boy. Noah Blake, a farmer's son in New England, began his diary on March 25, 1805, when his father gave him a diary for his fifteenth birthday. He wrote in it almost every day from March through December. It is found in *Eric Sloane's Sketches of America Past* (1986). Sloane found the leather-bound, wood-backed diary and the stone inkwell Noah used in an old house. Sloane's sketches of tools, furniture, the farm, and buildings, along with his explanations of Noah's entries, make this boy's life come alive. Students interested in tools and woodworking would especially appreciate this book. Noah writes a lot about all the construction they did on the farm and about his girlfriend, Sarah, which would interest students.

There are a number of diaries written by children that you can use with students who are learning about life in the 1800s. Charlotte Forten began her diary in 1854, when she was sixteen. It is in the 2000 book *A Free Black Girl Before the Civil War: The Diary of Charlotte Forten, 1854*. Charlotte attended a school in Salem, Massachusetts, where African American and white students were taught together. She writes about reading Charles Dickens and the poems of Phillis Wheatley. She describes how she reacted when a fugitive slave was returned to bondage, and tells of going to antislavery meetings.

Students who read *A Nineteenth-Century Schoolgirl: The Diary of Caroline Cowles Richards, 1852–1855*, can find out about transportation, clothing styles, games, and school subjects during this period of time. Caroline began her diary when she was ten. She lived with her grandparents in Canandaigua, New York. In addition to writing about daily activities, she describes her experience going to hear Susan B. Anthony speak and her attempt to change her grandmother's reaction.

> She talked very plainly about our rights and how we ought to stand up for them, and said the world would never go right until the women had just as much right to vote and rule as the men. She asked us all to come up and sign our names who would promise to do all in our power to bring about that glad day when equal rights should be the law of the land. . . . I could not make Grandmother agree with her at all. (Richards 2000, 24)

Robert E. Lee's daughter, Eleanor Agnes Lee, began a journal in 1852, when she was twelve. For five years she recorded vivid details about her experiences in getting an education and attending concerts, dress balls, and other social events, as well as about her daily life. She also wrote about the hours she spent teaching slaves and reflected on her spiritual growth and struggles with her conscience. Lee's journal is in *Growing Up in the 1850s* (1984).

I first heard about the diary of twelve-year-old Nettie Ketcham from a relative on Long Island who volunteered at the Ketcham Inn Foundation. After learning that it had been privately published, she sent me a copy. *Nettie's Diary: The 1800s*

Diary of Nettie Ketcham is noteworthy because it shows how the coming of the railroad affected this rural area of Long Island. Nettie began her diary in January 1881. By April, the Patchogue-to-Eastport extension of the railroad was being built through her backyard in the village of Center Moriches, New York. The first passenger train came through in July. The editor's foreword explains that "this was the period of time in this village when the transition from a rural agrarian lifestyle to one where travel by rail became possible" (Ketcham 1995, 5).

The majority of the selections in *Real American Girls Tell Their Own Stories* (Hoobler and Hoobler 1999) were written by girls living in the 1800s or by women who had been children then. Teachers who are interested in using more than these short excerpts can look in the text credits on the last page of the book to find the source of a particular diary, then locate it through a library system. The girls in this book come from a variety of backgrounds, economic levels, and geographic areas. They write about many of the topics that girls might write about today—friends, school, boys, getting in trouble, having fun, and becoming a woman. Through reading this and other diaries, your students will come to realize that they have much in common with the children who wrote them, even though their lives in the past were so different from today's.

Children Achieving in the Arts

In introducing students to children in history and to children today who are making a difference, it is important to include the contributions of those with special talents in the visual and performing arts. When we think of the contributions of children, our first thoughts may be of famous people whose genius was evident at a very young age. Dennis Fradin's, *Remarkable Children* (1987), includes chapters on Mozart, Picasso, Judy Garland, and Shirley Temple. In *We Were There, Too!* (2001), Phillip Hoose tells about Jackie Cooper's life as a child actor. Cooper became famous in 1930 at the age of eight when he played the lead role in the movie *Skippy*. Child movie stars are discussed and quoted in *Children at Work*, a primary source research book for students. Jackie Cooper described what it was like to be a movie star at so young an age:

> The longer I stayed on the set, the less time I had to spend in school. . . . But I never minded the work. It was make-believe. . . . So I'd go in and out of grammar school. . . . I didn't know that back there in the school yard, normal kids were having normal, and much healthier, fun (Cooper 1981, 37 in Deitch 2000, 43).

Another famous boy actor, Nathan Field, was born in 1587 in England. He performed in Shakespeare's plays in front of Queen Elizabeth I. Because of his talent, famous writers like Ben Jonson created parts for him. Information about

Nathan can be found in Fiona Macdonald's *A Child's Eye View of History*.

Phillip Hoose tells the story of Vinnie Ream, who became a talented sculptor in her early teens. I was fascinated by the photograph of her in Figure 6–5. Vinnie lived in Washington, D.C., during the Civil War and realized her dream of creating a sculpture of Lincoln. She spent many afternoons molding his likeness while he worked in his office. On April 14, 1865, she had just about finished. That night, Lincoln was shot. Congress awarded Vinnie a contract to complete the sculpture.

Wang Yani was born in Gongcheng, China, in 1975. She showed incredible talent in painting when she was only three years old. The first major exhibition of her paintings was held in Shanghai when she was four. The beautiful book *A Young Painter: The Life and Paintings of Wang Yani—China's Extraordinary Young Artist* has color photographs of her and her delightful paintings of nature, monkeys, cats, and other animals (Zhensun and Low 1991).

Growing Up in Distant Lands

I have always been fascinated by China and I share this interest with my students. Some of my earliest memories are of my grandmother telling me stories about her sister, who, when she was twenty-four, traveled by herself to China in 1908 to teach in a school for girls. My grandmother showed me photographs of great-aunt Eula Hensley with these little girls. When I was elementary school age, I used to go up into the attic and read Eula's letters describing her life in China and the lives of the girls she taught. She wrote about what they did in school, how quickly they learned, and how she loved them. She also wrote about the suffering of those whose parents still practiced binding girls' feet: "My heart simply bleeds when I see these women hobbling along the streets with bound feet and these precious little girls with their feet paining them so" (Hensley 1908). Through reading my great-aunt's letters and looking at photographs, I learned a little about these children who, from my perspective then, lived so long ago and so far away from Kentucky. I wanted to know more about them and their country. Because of my lifelong interest in China, when I was writing this book I searched for autobiographies of people who grew up there. I found some that might be of interest to students.

Jean Fritz is probably a familiar author to many students. Those who enjoy her books might be interested to know that she was born in China. She writes about her childhood in China in *Homesick: My Own Story* (1982). It was not until she was twelve that her family moved back to America, in 1927. Fritz's storytelling ability gives us a real sense of China during this period and what it was like being

Figure 6–5. Vinnie Ream with her sculpture of President Lincoln (courtesy of the Library of Congress, LC-USZ62-10284).

an American growing up there.

Ji Li Jiang was twelve years old when the Cultural Revolution started in 1966. In *Red Scarf Girl: A Memoir of the Cultural Revolution* (1997), she tells of the changes that occurred and how she and her family were affected. China was also in turmoil at the time Lu Chi Fa became an orphan when his parents died in 1944. *Double Luck: Memoirs of a Chinese Orphan* (2001) is the story of his struggles and his dream of coming to America.

If teachers or any of our students have a special interest in another country, it is enriching to build on that interest by locating information about the children in that country, both in the past and today. Sharing your own such interest and research is a fine way to model lifelong learning for your students. Connecting with young people from their special place of interest can help your students meet the National Council of Social Studies performance expectation of being able to "describe personal connections to place—as associated with community, nation, and world" (NCSS 1994, 37). In addition, it can help build a foundation for life-long learning.

Using the Resources

It is encouraging to know that it is possible to include real children in many of the themes and topics studied in elementary and middle schools. This chapter alone introduces children who could be added to a study of early civilizations, exploration, colonial life, life in the 1800s, transportation, change, technology, heroes and heroines, Washington, D.C., the U.S. presidents, or China. For example, two of my social studies methods students taught transportation in a fourth-grade classroom. In addition to a Cobblestone theme pack on transportation and other sources, they used the story of Hermine Jahns, who traveled on the first cross-country trip made by a woman driver, and discussed Kate Shelley's bravery in preventing a train from going over a bridge that was washed out in a storm.

Children living during the time period students are studying who contributed to the arts could be introduced in relation to the events of that period. For example, the sculptor Vinnie Ream would fit with a study of the Civil War or a study of national leaders. During the time she spent with Lincoln as she molded his likeness, she formed the impression that he was a man of sorrow, still recovering from the death of his son and often deep in thought. Vinnie wrote in her diary, "I think [at these times] he was with his generals on the battlefields" (Hoose 2001, 126). Shirley Temple's contribution could be tied in with a study of the Great Depression because her films were made during the 1930s when so many people were suffering. President Franklin D. Roosevelt was referring to Shirley Temple in 1935 when he said, "During this depression, when the spirit of the people is lower than at any other time, it is a splendid thing that for just fifteen cents an American can go to a movie and look at the smiling face of a baby and forget his trouble" (Gardiner 1989, 36).

Diaries written by children in the 1800s, before the Civil War, give us a picture of what life was like then from a variety of perspectives. The children who wrote these diaries were from different backgrounds, social and economic levels, and geographic areas. Noah Blake was the son of a farmer in New England. Charlotte Forten was a free black girl whose family members, successful sailmakers in Pennsylania, sent her to school in Salem, Massachusetts. Caroline Richards lived in western New York and was the daughter of a Presbyterian minister. Agnes Lee was the daughter of Robert E. Lee, and lived in Arlington, Virginia, and at West Point. If we add to these the diary of Sallie Hester, the covered wagon girl introduced in Chapter 2, and the recollections of the slaves and child laborers from this period who we met in Chapter 4, we have a diverse collection of resources for our students. Using a collection like this, rather than just a single resource, gives our students a more complete understanding of a historical period and helps develop their historical thinking. Levstik and Barton (1997) report that their research shows children fail to see the diversity in history, instead visualizing the past as a linear development. Levstik and Barton give examples of this kind of thinking, such as children thinking that everyone in the colonial era lived in log cabins or that people in the 1800s dressed in formal clothes all the time. They attribute this kind of thinking to teachers' failing to be consistent in exposing students to different perspectives and failing to emphasize diversity. Their research shows that when we emphasize diversity and conflicting perspectives, students make these aspects of life part of their historical understanding.

Creating Profiles

After reading what children wrote about their lives in the years before the Civil War, your students could design posters giving a profile of each child. Divide the class into groups and have each group construct a poster about a different child. To make sure that each poster is as complete a profile as possible, give your students guidelines similar to these:

1. Include the following about the boy or girl: name; age; date of diary; where he or she lived and a description of that place; what school subjects he or she studied; his or her activities, work, interests, concerns, problems, and ways of having fun; and what events in his or her immediate area, state, or nation may be recorded in the diary.

2. Draw a picture of the boy or girl. If there is no picture in the source, draw how you imagine he or she might have looked.
3. Illustrate some of the activities described in the source.
4. Draw pictures of the places where the boy or girl lived and worked.

Display the completed posters side-by-side to make it easy for your students to compare them. Posters like this can help them understand how different children lived back then, what they experienced, and what their concerns and interests were.

Writing a Multigenre Paper

There is enough information available about some of the historical children introduced in this chapter for students to do research about them. Tutankhamen, Pocahontas, children who lived in the White House, Sacagawea, Louis Braille, Kate Shelley, Agnes Lee, Jean Fritz, and the young artists discussed are all possible topics for a multigenre research paper. Camille Allen has written a book to guide teachers through the process of writing these papers. *The Multigenre Research Paper: Voice, Passion and Discovery in Grades 4–6* describes the multigenre paper by saying that "each piece in the paper utilizes a different genre, reveals one facet of the topic, and makes its own point" (Allen 2001, 2). The paper can be visualized as "a collage of writing and artistic expression with an overarching theme that engulfs and informs the reader" (2). Completed papers are shared in a variety of creative ways planned by the students. The presentations can include drama, music, costumes, props, displays, and artwork. I was delighted to find that the fifth-grade student's multigenre paper that Allen includes in the appendix of the book as an example was written on Sacagawea. The paper includes a two-page research report, several kinds of poems, an obituary, a fiction piece, an ad for people with wilderness skills to join the Lewis and Clark expedition, diary entries, a newspaper article, and a crossword puzzle. The student's artwork enhances the paper. I would love to have seen this student's presentation. I imagine her pretending to be Sacagawea, dressed like the drawing on the cover of her report.

Constructing Picture-Book Biographies

Constructing a picture-book biography might appeal to students who really like to draw and paint, and can be an interesting addition to unit activities. An incident such as the one where Theodore Roosevelt's son managed to sneak his brother's pony into the White House would make a delightful picture book. A good way to begin is to invite students to look at a variety of picture books about specific people to get a feel for the characteristics of picture books and to get them thinking about how they could make their own. *Tutankhamen's Gift* by Robert Sabuda is one of the many picture books they could examine. To create a picture book, students can work together or individually. They first make a list, in sequence, of what they want to show about the person. For example, a list for George Fred Tilton, who worked on a whaling ship, might read as follows:

1. George sees a notice that the *Union*, a whaler, is scheduled to depart New Bedford.
2. He goes to the ship.
3. He hides in the ship until after it leaves port.
4. He is discovered and brought to the captain.
5. He is put on a boat to row toward a whale.
6. The whale is harpooned.
7. The whale pulls the boat.
8. The whale is captured and hooked to the whaling ship.
9. George spends a day on a tropical island.
10. He returns to his family.

The children then paint or draw a scene for each of the things they listed, dividing the scenes among group members if this is a group project. For a story like George's, they might want to include a map of where he traveled. The children can then lay out their completed illustrations in order and plan what they will write to accompany each one. After they write the text, the children could arrange the book so that there's text opposite each painting. To protect the art, laminate the pages before binding them together in a book that can be shared, then placed in the classroom library.

Creating a profile or a picture-book biography to get to know their historical peers lets your students construct knowledge through both visual art and different forms of writing. This builds their understanding of a historical event or time period. In *History Workshop*, Karen Jorgensen points out that children can clarify their comprehension through historical drawing. She states, "I've observed children discovering new historical meaning as they draw" (Jorgensen 1993, 19). Many of us can make the same observation as our students write or engage in other activities. As teachers, we are aware of our students diversity of talents, abilities, interests, backgrounds, and needs, so we know the importance of offering all of our students alternative ways of constructing and expressing their learning.

Making Connections

To connect with children in the past, our students must determine their values, ideas, beliefs, and attitudes in addition to finding out what they did and what their lives were like. In *Doing History*, Levstik and Barton emphasize that students need to be aware of the beliefs and values of historical people in order to understand the reasons for their actions. As students become immersed in a period of history, they can explore these cultural aspects of the historical child's life in the context of that time period. When they read a child's diary or letters as well as what has been written about him or her, they can make inferences about what the child valued, believed, and thought. For example, students can infer that Sarah Forbes Bonetta, Charlotte Forten, Caroline Richards, and Agnes Lee valued education because there is a lot written about their schooling and their successes in learning. Sarah had definite ideas about the proper clothes to wear on different occasions, as evidenced, for example, by a letter she wrote requesting specific items of dress for her visits with the queen. Agnes' interest in educating slaves and her concern for blind people are mentioned in her diary. Caroline wrote in her diary her ideas about women's rights, and Charlotte voiced her reactions to slavery and to the treatment of fugitive slaves by northern people. We know that Noah Blake valued work and resourcefulness because his diary gives details about things that get built on the farm and his interest in them. These are only a few of the many inferences your students might draw from the resources they study.

Once your students complete their analysis of a historical child, they can list what they themselves value, then make comparisons between their values and the earlier child's. Finally, you could lead your students in discussing how the period in which we live may affect our values, attitudes, beliefs, and ideas. Teaching and learning in social studies "are powerful when they are value-based" (NCSS 1994, 166). Through making such comparisons, students begin to "develop critical sensitivities . . . regarding attitudes, values and behaviors of people in different historical contexts" (34).

Continuing the Search for Sources

This book describes only the beginning of my ongoing search for resources by and about children in history. I invite you and your students to continue the adventure with me, for it is a fascinating adventure. I have shared a few ways that I located certain sources. I use a number of other strategies, too. I include both juvenile and adult literature in all my searches. A good way to begin is to conduct a search through your local library system for published diaries, journals, and other primary sources by children who lived in the period you wish to study and for the autobiographies, memoirs, and recollections of adults who were children during that time. Some authors who have written books about their childhoods are Carl Sandburg (*Prairie-Town Boy*, 1953) and Cathy Young (*Growing Up in Moscow*, 1989). Then look for secondary sources—biographies of children living in that time and of adults who were children then. Biographies sometimes include photographs and excerpts from primary sources. In another search, locate books about children in general that are related to the theme, topic, or time period you are teaching. Books in this category include Freedman's *Immigrant Kids* and Peavy's *Frontier Children*. If possible, search a college or university library system, which will have wonderful sources available that may not be found in the local library system. Look for both books and journal articles. *Social Education, Social Studies and the Young Learner, The Social Studies, Cobblestone,* and *American Heritage* are just a few of the journals in which I have found primary sources by children.

Beyond the library are other possibilities. I have found primary sources in historical societies and museums that I visited on vacations. Your local historical society will have sources that your class can use in a study of your community's history. Many museums and historical societies can be contacted through the Internet. If you are studying whaling in New England and you aren't anywhere near Mystic Seaport, the New Bedford Whaling Museum, or the Martha's Vineyard Historical Society, look at their websites. The Library of Congress and the National Archives have many primary sources by children and photographs for a variety of time periods. I have found the NCSS publication *Surfing Social Studies: The Internet Book* to be very helpful for online searches.

It is important to involve our students in collecting primary sources by and about historical children. If you are studying a time period or event that adults in your community lived through, such as World War II or the civil rights movement; the history of your community; or a theme such as change over time or citizenship, your students can conduct an oral history project and collect their own primary sources focusing on childhood. Compiling these interviews in a book to be placed in the local and school libraries would provide a resource for future classes.

Your students could also search for letters, diaries, and photographs in their own family collections. Many families have photographs from earlier time periods, and some have letters, postcards, journals, or diaries that earlier family members wrote when they were children. They might be willing to let your class copy these resources to use in a collection for classroom use. Have your students ask their family members, neighbors, friends' families, and others if they have any of these items. Copies could be laminated and placed in files according to the time period in which they belong.

Through searching for primary sources by children and young people, our students experience what it means to be historians collecting firsthand accounts of a time period. When the accounts they collect were created by their historical peers, they begin to realize that history is also about them—that it is their story, too.

Epilogue: Students Making Contributions Today

Pocahontas. James Forten. Harriet Hanson. Frederick Douglass. Johnny Clem. Ruby Bridges. Elizabeth Eckford. Anne Frank. Iqbal Masih. Nikosi Johnson. These are just a few of the children introduced in this book. What wonderful peers our students have in history and today! Inspired and motivated by these young people, our students can make their contributions.

Preserving the Present for Future Young Historians

Children who kept diaries, like Ada Millington and William Bircher, or who wrote letters, like some of the boys in the Civil War, were unknowingly preserving history. What they wrote provided records that today help us understand their periods of history. Our students can make their own contribution to preserving history by keeping diaries. Some might feel that they have nothing of interest to say, as did Agnes Lee when she wrote on April 20, 1853, "The everyday life of a little school girl of twelve years is not startling." In fact it was interesting, and not just because Agnes was the daughter of Robert E. Lee. Everyday events written in the diaries of children, famous or not, are important to us today. In the introduction to the diary of Caroline Richards, an ordinary nineteenth-century schoolgirl, the editor notes that "what were everyday events to Caroline are meaningful pieces of history to us. . . . From her diary, we learn about school subjects, clothing styles, and transportation of that time. We also learn that ideas were changing about slavery and women's right" (Richards 2000, 7). We can help our students understand that what they have to say is important too, not only now, but to those in the future. Encourage your students to begin diaries and write in them regularly. Remind them to record the date before they write each entry. They can write not only about their daily activities, but also about their reactions to what is happening in their community, the nation, and the world that is of interest or concern to them. They can give their ideas about issues and problems, describe events they attend, or write about trips they take. The possibilities are endless.

Creating a time capsule is an interesting project for students. They can collect items and pictures that are representative of their own lives. They might write letters to the future describing their lives, activities, methods of transportation, events of interest, issues of concern, and whatever else is important to them. They could take photographs showing things that might be of interest to young people in the future. The students would then place all of these in a container to be opened sometime in the future.

When the students at Broad Meadows Middle School raised money to build a school for children in Pakistan, they wanted to help those children and to realize Iqbal's dream. They also wanted to be sure that Iqbal and what he had done would not be forgotten. Your students might do something on a smaller scale, to recognize or honor the achievements of others. What are the children and young people in their school and community doing to help others or to create a better community? If your students don't know of a young person to honor, they could take a survey in grades three and up in their school to find out what the students have done or are currently doing. They could then use the information from the survey to create a service honor role to be displayed in the school. A scrapbook with the honorees' photographs and a description of their contributions could be placed in the school library as a permanent record. Your students could also plan and hold an honors ceremony to recognize children and young people who are making contributions to the world.

Taking Action

Ron Adams, the teacher at Broad Meadows Middle School, reflected that when his students told him they wanted to build a school in Pakistan, he thought that they wouldn't be able to do it. However, he kept his thoughts to himself and helped them. To his amazement, the students persisted and did raise the money to realize their goal. Students who are motivated can accomplish extraordinary things, as the contemporary children introduced in this book demonstrate. Trevor Ferrell's campaign for the people who were homeless led to a thirty-three room boarding house for them. Students in Albuquerque, New Mexico, raised money to build a peace statue. Craig Kielburger founded Free the Children to help children in bondage. Nkosi Johnson and Ryan White combated prejudice and discrimination against people with AIDS.

In this book, I shared ideas about some ways our students can make their own contributions. These are only suggestions. As teachers, we can help our students become aware of needs and issues in the communities where we live, in our nation, and in the world. We can motivate them to take action by introducing them to children throughout history and today who have made and are making contributions. When our students become personally involved and believe that they have the power to make a difference, they can say with Elizabeth Eckford, one of the Little Rock Nine, "When you believe in something, even if you're afraid, you'll find a way to accomplish your goals" (Rochelle 1993, 21).

Bibliography

Abodaher, David J. 1990. *Youth in the Middle East: Voices of Despair*. New York: Franklin Watts. The author's personal journey through Lebanon, Israel, and Egypt, visiting families and talking with young people about living in war-torn areas.

Adler, David. 1993. *A Picture Book of Anne Frank*. New York: Holiday House.

————. 2000. *A Picture Book of Sacagawea*. New York: Holiday House.

Adler, Jeanne W., ed. 1998. *In the Path of War: Children of the American Revolution Tell Their Stories*. Peterborough, NH: Cobblestone Publishing. A collection of oral history materials from people who were children during this war.

Alleman, Tillie P. 1889. *At Gettysburg or What a Girl Saw and Heard of the Battle*. New York: W. Lake Borland. (Reprinted in 1994 by Stan Clark Military Books, Gettysburg, PA.) The firsthand account by a girl living in Gettysburg during the Civil War.

Allen, Camille A. 2001. *The Multigenre Research Paper: Voice, Passion, and Discovery in Grades 4–6*. Portsmouth, NH: Heinemann. Describes how teachers can engage students in writing research papers using a variety of kinds of writing.

American Federation of Teachers (AFT). 1999. *Lost Futures: The Problem of Child Labor*. Washington, DC: American Federation of Teachers. This kit contains a video on child labor and a teacher's guide with lesson plans, plays, stories, poems, and ideas for taking action.

Amstel, Marsha. 2000. *Sybil Ludington's Midnight Ride*. Minneapolis, MN: Carolrhoda Books. Amstel tells the story of Sybil's horseback ride to rouse American soldiers to fight British soldiers at Danbury, Connecticut.

Atkin, Beth S. 1993. *Voices from the Fields: Children of Migrant Farmworkers Tell Their Stories*. Boston: Little, Brown. Interviews and photographs give insight into the children's struggles.

Bachrach, Susan D. 1994. *Tell Them We Remember: The Story of the Holocaust*. Boston: Little, Brown. The author is a staff member of the United States Holocaust Museum and includes photographs and information from the museum.

Bartoletti, Susan C. 1996. *Growing Up in Coal Country.* Boston: Houghton Mifflin. Stories of children working in coal mines, frequently using their own voices.

————. 1999. *Kids on Strike!* Boston: Houghton Mifflin. How children went on strike to improve working conditions for child laborers.

Barton, Keith C. 2001. "A Picture's Worth: Analyzing Historical Photographs in the Elementary Grades." *Social Education* 65 (5): 278–283.

Barton, Keith C., and Linda Levstik. 1994. "Back When God Was Around and Everything: Elementary Children's Understanding of Historical Time." *American Educational Research Journal* 33: 419–454.

Bates, Daisy. 1962. *The Long Shadow of Little Rock: A Memoir.* New York: David McKay. The story of the struggle to integrate Central High School and the memoir of the life of the remarkable woman who led that struggle.

Beals, Melba Pattillo. 1994. *Warriors Don't Cry: A Searing Memoir of the Battle to Integrate Little Rock's Central High.* New York: Pocket Books. Melba Pattillo, one of the Little Rock Nine students, tells of her experiences with segregation as a child and gives a complete account of what happened during the integration.

Belcher-Hamilton, Lisa. 1989. "Samantha Smith Took Action." *Cobblestone* 10 (1): 6–9. Samantha's letter to Yuri Andropov, information about her trip to Russia, and her actions on behalf of peace.

Berk, Laura E. 1999. *Infants, Children, and Adolescents.* Boston: Allyn and Bacon.

Berlin, Ira, Marc Favreau, and Steven F. Miller, eds. 1998. *Remembering Slavery: African Americans Talk about Their Personal Experiences in Slavery and Freedom.* New York: The New Press.

Berry, Carrie. 2000. *A Confederate Girl: The Diary of Carrie Berry, 1864.* Mankato, MN: Blue Earth Books. Ten-year-old Carrie wrote in her diary for six months during the time when battles were being fought in the Atlanta area. Background information, suggested activities, and a time line are included.

Bircher, William. 2000. *A Civil War Drummer Boy: The Diary of William Bircher, 1861–1865.* Mankato, MN: Blue Earth Books. Fifteen-year-old William was a drummer with the Second Minnesota Regiment. Background information, suggested activities, and a time line are included.

Blos, Joan. 1985. "Perspectives on Historical Fiction." In *The Story of Ourselves,* edited by Michael Tunnell and Richard Ammon, 11–17. Portsmouth, NH: Heinemann.

Bolden, Tonya. 2001. *Tell All the Children Our Story: Memories and Mementos of Being Young and Black in America.* New York: Harry N. Abrams. Includes excerpts from diaries and memoirs, paintings, photographs, and other sources portraying what it was like being young and black in America.

Braun, Joseph A., and C. Frederick Risinger, eds. 1999. *Surfing Social Studies: The Internet Book.* Washington, DC: National Council for the Social Studies. This helpful NCSS bulletin 98 describes how teachers can use the Internet in teaching social studies and gives a multitude of web sources.

Bridges, Ruby. 1999. *Through My Eyes*. New York: Scholastic. Ruby Bridges' own story of integrating William Frantz Public School, with photographs and other primary sources.

Brill, Marlene Targ. 1993. *Allen Jay and the Underground Railroad*. Minneapolis: Carolrhoda Books. The true story of how eleven-year-old Allen Jay helped a runaway slave, told simply for young readers.

Brimmer, Larry D. 1991. *A Migrant Family*. Minneapolis: Lerner. Photographs and the story of twelve-year-old Juan Medina and his family.

Brooks, Elisha. 1922. *A Pioneer Mother of California*. San Francisco: Harr Wagner.

Brophy, Jere, and Bruce VanSledright. 1997. *Teaching and Learning History in Elementary Schools*. New York: Teachers College Press.

Brown, Cynthia Stokes. 1994. *Connecting with the Past: History Workshop in Middle and High Schools*. Portsmouth, NH: Heinemann.

Bruchac, Joseph. 2000. *Sacagawea*. San Diego, CA: Silver Whistle.

Burroughs, Jean M. 1981. "Nettie's Big Fish." *Cobblestone* 2 (12): 34–37. Burroughs' story in this December issue is based on nine-year-old Nettie's diary about traveling on the Oregon Trail. It includes an excerpt from her diary.

Carter, Jimmy. 2001. *An Hour Before Daylight: Memories of a Rural Boyhood*. New York: Simon and Schuster. The former president describes his childhood in Georgia in the 1930s.

Ciardiello, Angelo Vincent. 2001. "Tolerance and Forgiveness: An Interdisciplinary Lesson on Civic Efficacy." *Social Studies and the Young Learner* 14 (1): 26–29. Outlines a two-period lesson for grade three on the integration of schools, using the experience of Ruby Bridges.

Cloughley, Dorothea E. 1993. "Trevor's Campaign for the Homeless." *Cobblestone* 14 (10): 11–15. This December issue on children's contributions includes a story about eleven-year-old Trever Ferrell who campaigned to help the homeless.

Cobblestone, Publisher. 1999. *Appleseeds: Children of Ancient Egypt*. 1 (6). This entire February issue on children of ancient Egypt includes an article about Tutankhamen, the boy king.

————. 1981. *Cobblestone: The Industrial Revolution* 2 (9). This entire September 1981 issue is devoted to the Industrial Revolution and includes several articles on child labor.

————. 1989. *Cobblestone: Frederick Douglass*. 10 (2). This entire February 1989 issue features Frederick Douglass and includes an excerpt from his autobiography telling about his efforts to learn to read.

————. 1992. *Cobblestone: History of Labor*. 13 (8). This October issue features the history of labor and includes information about child labor and photographs by Lewis Hine.

————. 2001. *Cobblestone: Mill Girls*. 22 (3). This March issue, devoted to the Lowell mill girls, includes details about their work and the factories, their lives, the *Lowell Offering*, and a song the girls sang.

————. 1999. *Cobblestone: Children in the Civil War*. 20 (9). This December issue contains articles and activities about children in this war.

————. 1989. *Cobblestone: Children Who Shaped History*. 10 (1). This entire January issue features children who have taken action in the past and recently.

————. 1993. *Cobblestone: Kid Power, Changing Public Policy*. 14 (10). This December issue is on ways children have made contributions and gives ideas for taking action.

————. 1998. *Cobblestone: Orphan Trains*. 19 (4). This April issue about the orphan trains includes an interview with a former orphan train rider.

————. 2002. *Cobblestone: Faces: World Refugees*. 19 (1). This entire September issue contains articles and activities related to refugees.

————. 1994. *World War II*. Peterborough, NH: Cobblestone. This theme pack includes nine issues of *Cobblestone* related to World War II, and a teacher's guide.

Coer, Eleanor. 1977. *Sadako and the Thousand Paper Cranes*. New York: Dell. The story of a twelve-year-old girl who died of radiation from the atom bomb that was dropped on Hiroshima when she was two. She began folding paper cranes after a friend told her that the gods would make her well if she folded a thousand. Her friends folded the remaining number after she died.

Coggins, Jack. 1967. *Boys in the Revolution: Young Americans Tell Their Part in the War for Independence*. Harrisburg, PA: Stackpole Books. This book has excerpts from the diaries and journals of John Greenwood, Ebenezer Fox, Joseph Martin, and many others.

Cohen, Barbara. 1982. *Gooseberries to Oranges*. New York: Lothrop, Lee, and Shepard Books. The true story of eight-year-old Fanny, who came from eastern Europe to America. Includes her experiences aboard ship and on Ellis Island.

Cohen, Robert. 1996. "Dear Mrs. Roosevelt: Cries for Help from Depression Youth" and "To Mrs. Roosevelt, Who 'Looks for the Poor': A Primary Source Teaching Segment." *Social Education* 60 (5): 271–276, 295. Teaching ideas and excerpts from letters written to Eleanor Roosevelt from the Roosevelt papers at the Franklin D. Roosevelt Presidential Library, Hyde Park, New York.

Cohen, Rose. 1995. *Out of the Shadow: A Russian Jewish Girlhood on the Lower East Side*. Ithaca, NY: Cornell University Press. Cohen tells the story of her life as a child living in Russia, coming to America, and working in a sweatshop to pay for the rest of her family to come.

Coles, Robert. 1995. *The Story of Ruby Bridges*. New York: Scholastic. In this movingly illustrated book, Coles, who met with Ruby when she integrated William Frantz School, portrays her faith and courage.

————. 1995. *Their Eyes Meeting the World: Listening to Children: The Drawings and Paintings of Children*. Boston: Houghton Mifflin. Artwork by Ruby Bridges is found on pages ten and eleven.

Collett, James. 1989. "Drummer Boys." *Cobblestone*. 10 (1): 10–13.

Colman, Penny. 2000. *Girls: A History of Growing Up Female in America*. New York: Scholastic. Histories of girls growing up in different regions and historical periods, including photographs; excerpts from diaries, letters, and memoirs; and other primary sources.

Coombs, Karen M. 2000. *Children of the Dust Days*. Minneapolis: Carolrhoda Books. Photographs of children with text explaining this period of history. This book is one of many in Carolrhoda's Picture the American Past series featuring children in history.

Cooper, Jackie. 1981. *Please Don't Shoot My Dog: The Autobiography of Jackie Cooper, With Dick Kleiner*. New York: William Morrow.

Cooper, Michael L. 1999. *Indian School: Teaching the White Man's Way*. New York: Clarion Books. Includes quotes from people who were students at the Carlisle Indian School and a number of photographs.

Cox, Deborah. 2000. "The Antebellum South: Fifth Graders' Understanding of History." *Social Studies and the Young Learner* 13 (2): 17–19. Describes using resources that are from the perspective of children and analyzes students' interpretations of those sources.

Cunningham, Ann Marie. 1993. "Candle in the Wind: The Life and Legacy of Ryan White." *Cobblestone* 14 (10): 4–10.

Currie, Stephen. 1997. *We Have Marched Together: The Working Children's Crusade*. Minneapolis: Lerner Publications. Currie describes child labor and focuses on the child workers protest march led by Mother Jones.

Damuni, Aida Hasan. 2002. "A Massacre to Our Hearts." *Faces* 19 (1): 33–35. This entire issue of Cobblestone's *Faces* is on refugees. In this article about Palestinian refugees, four young teens tell about their lives in the Shatila camp.

David, Rosalie. 1994. *Growing Up in Ancient Egypt*. Mahwah, NJ: Troll Associates. Describes children's lives in ancient Egypt with a section on Tutankhamen.

Dean, Patricia. 1984. "Children in Montana." *Montana, The Magazine of Western History* 34 (winter): 38–41.

Deitch, JoAnne W., ed. 2000a. *Children at Work: Researching American History*. Carlisle, MA: Discovery Enterprises. Primary sources on child labor including a song, the testimony from an injured child worker, and an essay written by a mill girl for the *Lowell Offering* magazine. Includes recollections of child movie stars in the thirties.

————. 2001. *Get a Clue! An Introduction to Primary Sources*. Carlisle, MA: Discovery Enterprises. Introduces students to primary sources and provides practice pages for developing skill in using them.

————. 1998. *The Lowell Mill Girls: Life in the Factory*. Carlisle, MA: Discovery Enterprises. One of the primary source books in the Perspectives on History series.

————. 2000b. *Woman's Suffrage: Researching American History*. Carlisle, MA: Discovery Enterprises. Primary sources present the struggle for women's rights. Notes are included to help students understand the sources.

Delisle, Jim. 1991. *Kid Stories: Biographies of Twenty Young People You'd Like to Know.* Minneapolis: Free Spirit. Children and youth who are making a difference today.

DeVoto, Bernard, ed. 1953. *The Journals of Lewis and Clark.* Boston: Houghton Mifflin Co.

Dewey, John. 1934. *Art as Experience.* New York: Capricorn Books, G. P. Putnam's Sons.

Diouf, Sylviane A. 2001. *Growing Up in Slavery.* Brookfield, CT: The Millbrook Press. Describes the lives of children who were slaves and includes photographs, the recollections of former slaves, and other primary sources.

Donnelly, Judy. 1988. *Tut's Mummy Lost . . . and Found.* New York: Random House. The discovery of Tutankhamen's tomb with photographs of some of the treasures found there.

Douglass, Frederick. 1994. *Escape from Slavery: The Boyhood of Frederick Douglass in His Own Words.* New York: Alfred A. Knopf. An edited version of Douglass' autobiography of his early years.

————. 1982. *Narrative of the Life of Frederick Douglass, An American Slave, Written by Himself.* New York: Penguin Books. One of a number of editions published since 1845.

Douty, Esther. 1968. *Forten the Sailmaker.* New York: Rand McNally. The story of James Forten, a free African American who became a privateer during the American Revolution and later a successful sailmaker in Philadelphia.

Downey, Matthew T. 1986. "Teaching the History of Childhood." *Social Education* (April/May): 261–267. Discusses the advantages of teaching about children in history.

Earle, Alice Morse, ed. 1974. *Diary of Anna Green Winslow: A Boston School Girl of 1771.* Boston: Houghton Mifflin. Twelve-year-old Anna's diary is one of the few children's diaries surviving from this time period.

Eastman, Charles A. 1971(1902). *Indian Boyhood.* 1902 Reprint, New York: Dover. This is Eastman's autobiography of his childhood with his Sioux relatives.

Edinger, Monica. 2000. *Seeking History: Teaching with Primary Sources in Grades 4–6.* Portsmouth, NH: Heinemann.

Eggen, Paul, and Don Kauchak. 2001. *Educational Psychology: Windows on Classrooms,* 5th ed. Upper Saddle River, NJ: Merrill/Prentice Hall.

Eisner, Elliot W. 2002. *The Arts and the Creation of the Mind.* New Haven: Yale University Press.

Epstein, Rachel. 1997. *Anne Frank.* New York: Franklin Watts. Epstein tells Anne's story and includes some excerpts from her diary.

Etkin, Linda, and Bebe Willoughby. 1992. *America's Children: Real-Life Stories and Poems About Children, Past and Present.* New York: Western Publishing. Contains primary sources and true stories of children from colonial times through the late 1900s.

Eyes on the Prize (1954–1965). 1987. PBS 424, Blackside Inc. Videocassettes. Produced and directed by Judith Vecchione, edited by Daniel Eisenberg. The first videocassette in this series of six, *Fighting Back: 1957–1962*, begins by showing Ruby Bridges entering school with a guard and continues with the Little Rock Nine, the nine students who integrated Central High. This videocassette series can be checked out through many local public library systems.

Fa, Lu Chi, with Becky White. 2001. *Double Luck: Memoirs of a Chinese Orphan*. New York: Holiday House. Lu Chi Fa tells of his hardships growing up as an orphan during a time of political turmoil in China.

Feldman, Ruth Tenzer. 1993. "The Supreme Court Needs You!" *Cobblestone*. 14 (10): 27–31. Includes information about the three children in the case *Tinker v. Des Moines*.

Ferrell, Frank, Janet Ferrell, and Edward Wakin. 1990. *Trevor's Place: The Story of the Boy Who Brings Hope to the Homeless*. New York: HarperCollins.

Fertig, Gary. 2000. "Hard Times and New Deals: Teaching Fifth Graders About the Great Depression." *Social Education* 65 (1): 34–40. Background, teaching ideas, and a copy of a letter from a fifth grader.

Filipović, Zlata. 1994. *Zlata's Diary: A Child's Life in Sarajevo*. New York: Viking. When Zlata began her diary at age ten, there was peace. As war began and continued, she wrote about the danger, violence, and struggles she faced daily.

Fisher, Leonard E. 1986. *Ellis Island: Gateway to the New World*. New York: Holiday House. Information about Ellis Island and photographs of immigrant children.

Fleischner, Jennifer. 1997. *I Was Born a Slave: The Story of Harriet Jacobs*. Brookfield, CT: Millbrook Press. Includes selections from Jacob's autobiography.

Forten, Charlotte. 2000. *A Free Black Girl before the Civil War: The Diary of Charlotte Forten, 1854*. Mankato, MN: Blue Earth Books. Sixteen-year-old Charlotte's life in a boarding school, concerns about a fugitive slave, and involvement in the anti-slavery movement.

Fox, Anne, and Abraham Podietz. 1998. *Ten Thousand Children: True Stories Told by Children Who Escaped on Kindertransport*. West Orange, NJ: Behrman House. Recollections of adults who escaped to England on the Kindertransport trains during World War II.

Fradin, Dennis B. 2000. *Bound for the North Star: True Stories of Fugitive Slaves*. New York: Clarion Books. Includes the story of Ann Maria Weems, a fifteen-year-old slave who escaped to the north.

———. 1987. *Remarkable Children: Twenty Who Made History*. Boston: Little, Brown. Stories of children from different time periods who made extraordinary contributions to history.

Frank, Anne. 1952. *Anne Frank: The Diary of a Young Girl*. New York: Doubleday.

Frank, John. 2001. *The Tomb of the Boy King*. New York: Frances Foster Books/ Farrar, Straus, and Giroux. The story of the discovery of Tutankhamen's tomb is told as a narrative poem.

Freedman, Russell. 1983. *Children of the Wild West*. New York: Clarion Books. A must-have book full of photographs and quotes from people recalling their childhoods going to or in the West.

———. 1992. *Immigrant Kids*. New York: Scholastic. Another must-have book with quotes from immigrants' memoirs and many photographs.

———. 1994. *Kids at Work: Lewis Hine and the Crusade Against Child Labor*. New York: Clarion Books. Hine's photographs and information about child labor.

———. 1997. *Out of Darkness: The Story of Louis Braille*. New York: Clarion Books. Louis Braille's childhood and how he invented a way for people who are blind to read.

Freiberg, H. Jerome and Amy Driscoll. 1996. *Universal Teaching Strategies*. 2nd ed. Boston: Allyn and Bacon. Chapter 12 contains ideas for role play, simulation, and drama.

French, Barsina Rogers. "Diary, 1867." Manuscript diary. San Marino, CA: The Huntington Library.

Fresch, Eula. 2001. "Children Empowering Children in Working for Peace and Justice." *Trends and Issues*. (summer): 4–6.

———. 2002. "Connecting Children with Children in History Using Primary Sources." *Southern Social Studies Journal*. (summer): 38–49.

Fritz, Jean. 1982. *Homesick: My Own Story*. New York: A Yearling Book/Dell Publishing. Jean Fritz writes about her childhood in China and her return to America in 1927 when she was twelve.

Gardiner, Harry. 1989. "Shirley Temple: Child Star." *Cobblestone* 10 (1): 36–38. In this January issue on children's contributions to history, Gardiner writes about Shirley Temple's talents and the effect her movies had on people in the 1930s.

Gardner, Howard. 1993. *Multiple Intelligences: The Theory in Practice*. New York: Basic Books.

Gillespie, Sarah. 2000. *A Pioneer Farm Girl: The Diary of Sarah Gillespie, 1877–1878*. Mankato, MN: Blue Earth Books. Excerpts from Sarah's diary, with explanations and activities for students.

Graff, Nancy. 1993. *Where the River Runs: A Portrait of a Refugee Family*. Boston: Little, Brown. Photographs and the story of three boys and their family who came from Cambodia and adjusted to a new life in Massachusetts.

Green, Laura O. 1992. *Child Labor: Then and Now*. New York: Franklin Watts. A history of child labor, beginning with the Industrial Revolution in Britain.

Greenfeld, Howard. 1993. *The Hidden Children*. New York: Ticknor & Fields. Stories of and excerpts from the writings of Jewish children who were sent away from their homes to escape the Nazis.

Greenfield, Eloise, and Lessie Jones Little. 1979. *Childtimes: A Three-Generation Memoir*. New York: Scholastic. Three African American women tell about their childhoods.

Halbfinger, David N. 2003. "Birmingham Recalls a Time When Children Led the Fight." *New York Times*, 2 May, sec. A1, p. 29. Adults recall their experiences as children during the 1960s.

Hampsten, Elizabeth. 1991. *Settlers' Children: Growing Up on the Great Plains*. Norman, OK: University of Oklahoma Press. Memoirs and letters by people who were children of settlers.

Harding, Priscilla. 1985. "Growing Up in World War II." *Cobblestone* 6 (12): 10–13. Harding's experiences as a child during this war.

Harvey, Brett. 1986. *My Prairie Year: Based on the Diary of Elenore Plaisted*. New York: Holiday House. Plaisted's recollection of being a nine-year-old in the West in 1889 is told in story form with illustrations.

Harvey, Stephanie. 1998. *Nonfiction Matters: Reading, Writing and Research in Grades 3–8*. York, ME: Stenhouse Publishers. Strategies for in-depth learning using nonfiction.

Haskins, Jim. 1993. *Get on Board: The Story of the Underground Railroad*. New York: Scholastic. Includes a chapter on the songs of the Underground Railroad.

Hensley, Eula W. 1908. Family letters from China.

Hester, Sallie. 2000. *A Covered Wagon Girl: The Diary of Sallie Hester, 1849–1850*. Mankato, MN: Blue Earth Books. Excerpts from this fourteen-year-old girl's diary tell of her trip on the Oregon-California trail.

Hickey, M. Gail. 1999. *Bringing History Home: Local and Family History Projects for Grades K–6*. Needham Heights, MA: Allyn and Bacon. Activities and resources for teachers doing family history.

Hodges, Elaine P. 1998. *Seneca Falls: Achieving Woman's Rights*. Peterborough, NH: Cobblestone. This is one of the resources in Cobblestone's Teaching with Primary Sources series. Included in this volume is information about Elizabeth Cady Stanton's childhood concern for women's rights.

Holland, Ruth. 1970. *Mill Child*. New York: The Macmillan Co. Although the title refers to mill children, Holland covers child labor in America and includes testimonies of child workers.

Holliday, Laurel. 1999. *Children of the Dream: Our Own Stories of Growing Up Black in America*. New York: Pocket Books. Thirty-eight African Americans share their stories.

Hoobler, Dorothy and Thomas Hoobler. 1995. *The African American Family Album*. New York: Oxford University Press. This book in the American Family Albums series uses photographs, memorabilia, and primary sources to tell the story of African Americans from life in Africa to life in America today.

————. 1994a. *The Chinese American Family Album*. New York: Oxford University Press.

————. 1994b. *The Italian American Family Album*. New York: Oxford University Press.

————. 1994c. *The Mexican American Family Album*. New York: Oxford University Press.

————. 1999. *Real American Girls Tell Their Own Stories*. New York: Atheneum. Selections from girls' diaries across two centuries, including an entry from the diary of Martha Carey Thomas, who later became a suffrage leader.

————. 1997. *The Scandinavian American Family Album*. New York: Oxford University Press.

Hoople, Cheryl G. 1978. *As I Saw It: Women Who Lived the American Adventure*. New York: The Dial Press. Includes accounts by Virginia Reed Murphy of her winter with the Donner party trapped in the Sierras as a child; by Zitkala-Sa of her experiences at Carlisle Indian School; and by Delfina Cuero of being forced to keep moving further into the San Diego hill country with her family to escape going to a reservation.

Hoose, Phillip. 1993. *It's Our World, Too! Stories of Young People Who Are Making a Difference*. Boston: Little, Brown & Co.

————. 2001. *We Were There, Too! Young People in U.S. History*. New York: Melanie Kroupa Books/Farrar Straus Giroux. I can't praise this book enough! Photographs and other primary sources illustrate and describe the lives of children and young people in America's history.

Huftalen, Sarah Gillespie. 1993. *All Will Yet Be Well: The Diary of Sarah Gillespie Huftalen, 1873–1952*. Iowa City, Iowa: University of Iowa Press. Sarah includes many details about her life as a farm girl in this diary, begun when she was eleven.

Hurmence, Belinda. 1997. *Slavery Time When I Was Chillun*. New York: G. P. Putnam. People who were slaves when they were children describe their lives in slavery. Photographs are included.

Hyatt, Patricia Rusch. 1995. *Coast to Coast with Alice*. Minneapolis, MN: Carolrhoda Books, Inc. Fictional diary about sixteen-year-old Hermine Jahns' 1909 ride across the country in an automobile driven by Alice Ramsey.

Irvine, Elizabeth. 1994. "Teenage Prisoner of War." *Cobblestone* 15 (1): 12–14. Irvine was a prisoner of war in the Philippines during the Japanese occupation..

Jackdaw. 2001. *American Indians: Early Boarding Schools*. Amawalk, NY: Jackdaw Publications. This and the following Jackdaw listings are the Jackdaw Photo Collections which include twelve, seventeen by twenty-two inch photographs with captions, a photo-analysis sheet, and other resources.

————. 1997a. *Child Labor: The Shame of the Nation*. A photo collection of Lewis Hine's child labor photographs.

————. 1999a. *Civil War: Young Soldiers*.

————. 1997b. *The Depression Hits Home*.

————. 2001. *The Dust Bowl*.

————. 1997c. *Ellis Island: The Immigrants' Experience*.

————. 1999b. *Holocaust Children*.

————. 1999c. *Japanese-American Internment: Life in the Camps*.

————. 2000. *Woman Suffrage: The Fight for Equality*. Photo number 7, taken in Washington in 1913, shows children with balloons participating in one of the "living history" scenes the movement liked to create to further the cause.

————. 1999d. *World War II: The War at Home*.

Jacobs, Harriet A. 2000. (1861). *Incidents in the Life of a Slave Girl Written by Herself*. Cambridge: Harvard University Press.

Jeffries, Alonzo. 1863. *Diary Manuscript*. Chester County Historical Society, West Chester, PA.

Jernegan, Laura. 2000. *A Whaling Captain's Daughter: The Diary of Laura Jernegan, 1868–1871*. Mankato, MN: Blue Earth Books. Laura experiences living on her father's ship. She describes whale hunts, whale oil processing, her schooling, and other activities on the ship.

Jiang, Ji Li. 1997. *Red Scarf Girl: A Memoir of the Cultural Revolution*. New York: Harper Collins. The difficulties Ji Li faced as a young girl growing up in China during the Cultural Revolution.

Jorgensen, Karen L. 1993. *History Workshop: Reconstructing the Past with Elementary Students*. Portsmouth, NH: Heinemann. Jorgensen describes her process approach for helping children create historical meaning.

Joyce, Bruce, and Weil, Marsha. 1996. *Models of Teaching*, 5th ed. Boston: Allyn and Bacon.

Karnes, Frances A., and Suzanne M. Bean. 1993. *Girls and Young Women Leading the Way: Twenty True Stories About Leadership*. Minneapolis, MN: Free Spirit. What twenty girls did to bring about change. Includes many suggestions for what other young people can do.

Ketcham, Nettie. 1995. *Nettie Ketcham: The 1880's Diary of Nettie Ketcham*. Moriches, NY: Ketcham Inn Foundation. Nettie describes her daily activities living on Long Island in the 1880s.

Kielburger, Craig. 1998. *Free the Children: A Young Man Fights Against Child Labor and Proves That Children Can Change the World*. New York: Harper Perennial.

Killion, Ronald, and Charles Walker, eds. 1973. *Slavery Time When I Was Chillun Down on Marster's Plantation*. Savannah: Beehive Press. Contains interviews conducted through the Federal Writers' Project of former Georgia slaves who were children when slavery ended in 1865.

King, Casey, and Linda B. Osborne. 1997. *Oh, Freedom! Kids Talk About the Civil Rights Movement with the People Who Made It Happen*. New York: Alfred A. Knopf. Thirty-one interviews that children conducted, with many photographs.

King, David C. 1999. *Civil War Days: Discover the Past with Exciting Projects, Games, Activities and Recipes*. New York: John Wiley and Sons, Inc. One of the books in the American Kids in History series with many teacher resources.

—————, ed. 1997. *The Dust Bowl: Perspectives on History Series*. Carlisle, MA: Discovery Enterprises. Primary sources about this period of history.

—————. 2000. *World War II Days: Discover the Past with Exciting Projects, Games, Activities, and Recipes*. New York: John Wiley and Sons. One of the books in the American Kids in History series.

King Jr., Martin Luther. 1960. "The Burning Truth in the South." *The Progressive*. May: 8–10. In the article, Dr. King praises the courage of students for their courage in integrating schools.

Knight, P. T. 1993. *Primary Geography, Primary History*. London: David Fulton. About children in history.

Koetsch, Peg. 1994. "Museum-in-Progress: Student-Generated Learning Environments." *Social Studies and the Young Learner* 7 (1): 15–18, 32.

Kuklin, Susan. 1998. *Iqbal Masih and the Crusaders Against Child Slavery*. New York: Henry Holt. The story of Iqbal's bondage working in a carpet factory in Pakistan, how he became free and helped others to escape, and the impact of his life.

Larcom, Lucy. 1986. *A New England Girlhood: Outlined from Memory*. Boston: Northeastern University Press. Larcom's childhood in Beverly, Massachusetts, her years working in the mill at Lowell, and her early adulthood.

—————. 1970 (1875). *An Idyl of Work*. Westport, CT: Greenwood Press. Larcum's narrative poem about women's factory life in Lowell about 1845.

Lavelle, Robert. 1992. "Documentary Films, Educational Technology, and *Eyes on the Prize*." *Social Education* 56 (5): 345–348. Ideas for how teachers can use documentary films.

Lawlor, Veronica. 1995. *I Was Dreaming to Come to America: Memories from the Ellis Island Oral History Project*. New York: Viking. Recollections of people, most of whom came through Ellis Island as children. Contains collages illustrating each memoir and biographical information.

Lee, Agnes. 1984. *Growing Up in the 1850s: The Journal of Agnes Lee*. Chapel Hill: The University of North Carolina Press. Agnes Lee writes about fancy balls, weddings, concerts, schooling, and her struggles with her conscience.

Lee, Mary Piak. 1990. *Quiet Odyssey: A Pioneer Korean Woman in America*. Seattle: University of Washington Press.

Leiner, Katherine. 1996. *First Children: Growing Up in the White House*. New York: Tambourine Books. The lives of children in seventeen first families with photographs and archival illustrations.

Leotta, Joan, and Beth Haverkamp. 1993. "Recording the Voice: The National Archives." *Cobblestone*. 14 (10): 40–42. Information about the purpose of the National Archives and the types of records preserved there. Includes letters children have written to leaders.

Lester, Julius. 1998. *To Be a Slave*. New York: Puffin Books. In this Newbery Honor book, former slaves tell about their lives, including recollections about their childhoods.

Levine, Ellen. 1993. *Freedom's Children: Young Civil Rights Activists Tell Their Own Stories*. New York: Puffin Books. The most complete source I have found of the recollections of people who were involved in the civil rights movement when they were young. Includes photographs of the children and of some of the events.

Levstik, Linda S., and Keith C. Barton. 1996. "They Still Use Some of Their Past: Historical Salience in Elementary Children's Chronological Thinking." *Journal of Curriculum Studies* 28: 531–576.

———. 1997. *Doing History: Investigating with Children in Elementary and Middle Schools*. Mahwah, NJ: Lawrence Erlbaum Associates. A valuable reference and resource with many vignettes for history teachers.

Lewis, Barbara. 1998. *The Kids Guide to Social Action: How to Solve the Social Problems You Choose—and Turn Creative Thinking into Positive Action*. Minneapolis: Free Spirit. The author features young people who are making a difference and gives ideas and resources for students to use as guides for taking action.

Listen to Children: A Moral Journey with Robert Coles. 1995. Social Media Productions. Videocassette. Includes short news clips of Ruby Bridges entering William Franz School.

Littlefield, Holly. 2001. *Children of the Indian Boarding Schools*. Minneapolis: Carolrhoda Books. A Picture the American Past series book with photographs and information about these children.

Loeper, John J. 1999. *Meet the Allens in Whaling Days*. New York: Benchmark Books. The Allens were a real whaling family that lived on Nantucket Island in the first half of the 1800s. This story shows what life might have been like for children then.

Low-Beer, A., and J. Blyth. 1983. *Teaching History to Younger Children*. London: The Historical Association.

Lyons, Mary. 1992. *Letters from a Slave Girl: The Story of Harriet Jacobs*. New York: Charles Scribner's Sons. Historical fiction that uses letters to tell Jacobs' life.

Macdonald, Fiona. 1998. *A Child's Eye View of History: Discover History Through the Experiences of Children from the Past*. New York: Simon and Schuster Books for Young Readers. Uses diaries, letters, interviews, and other evidence to tell the stories of real children from the past.

Marten, James. 1998. *The Children's Civil War*. Chapel Hill, NC: University of North Carolina Press. Provides information about how the Civil War affected children.

Martin, Joseph P. 2001. *The Diary of Joseph Plumb Martin, A Revolutionary War Soldier*. New York: Benchmark Books. From the In My Own Words series, Joseph's account of his years serving in the war.

Marx, Trish. 1994. *Echoes of World War II*. Minneapolis, MN: Lerner. Stories of six children who grew up in different parts of the world during World War II.

McAuley, Eliza Ann. 1852. *Diary Manuscript*. Sacramento, CA State Library. Reprinted in Kenneth L. Holmes, ed. 1985, *Covered Wagon Women*, Vol. 4. Glendale, CA: Arthur H. Clark.

McCully, Emily A. 1996. *The Bobbin Girl*. New York: Dial Books for Young Readers. A picture book portraying the life of a young girl in a cotton mill, inspired by an incident from the life of Harriet Hanson.

McDaniel, Kate Furniss. 1853. *From Prairie to Pacific: A Narrative of a Trip Across the Plains of a Family from Illinois with a Covered Wagon and Oxen*. Edited by Mai Luman Hill. Typescript 9CBF98. Sacramento: California State Library.

McNeil, Donald G. 2001. "South Africa's Small Warrior Against AIDS Dies Quietly." *New York Times*, 2 June, A3.

Mellon, James, ed. 1988. *Bullwhip Days, The Slaves Remember: An Oral History*. New York: Weidenfeld and Nicholson.

Meltzer, Milton. 1994. *Cheap Raw Material*. New York: Viking. Story of child labor past and present. Includes the voices of young workers.

————. 1993. "Voices from the Past." In *The Story of Ourselves: Teaching History Through Children's Literature*, edited by Michael Tunnell and Richard Ammon, 27–30. Portsmouth, NH: Heinemann. Meltzer, author of numerous juvenile books, gives his approach to writing history.

Millington, Ada. 1977. "Journal Kept While Crossing the Plains, 1862." *Southern California Quarterly* 59 (summer): 13–48. Includes an introduction and explanations of the text by Charles Clarke.

Moore, Kay. 1994. *If You Lived at the Time of the Civil War*. New York: Scholastic.

Morris, Ann. 1994. *Dancing to America*. New York: Dutton Children's Books. The story, with color photos, of Anton Pankevich, a boy who came with his family to New York seeking freedom and began to fulfill his dream of becoming a ballet dancer.

Mulvaney, Katie. 2003. "Muslim Family Finding Peace, and Prejudice, in the Suburbs." *Providence Journal*, 27 May, B1, 6.

Murphy, Jim. 1990. *The Boys' War: Confederate and Union Soldiers Talk About the Civil War*. New York: Clarion Books. Excerpts from firsthand accounts of young soldiers and drummers. Includes photographs.

Myers, Walter Dean. 1999. *At Her Majesty's Request: An African Princess in Victorian England*. New York: Scholastic. The fascinating biography of Sarah Forbes Bonetta who at age seven was taken to England, where Queen Victoria provided for her care.

Myres, Sandra L., ed. 1980. *Ho for California! Women's Overland Diaries from the Huntington Library*. San Marino, CA: Henry E. Huntington Library and Art Gallery. One chapter is "Harriet Bunyard: Diary of a Young Girl." Although Harriet was nineteen, her diary would be interesting to compare with those written by younger people, especially since she wrote almost daily from May through October.

National Council for the Social Studies (NCSS). 1994. *Expectations of Excellence: Curriculum Standards for Social Studies*. Washington, DC: National Council for the Social Studies.

Newman, Shirlee P. 2000. *Child Slavery in Modern Times*. New York: Franklin Watts. Explains how children around the world are used as slaves or child laborers and describes actions that young people are taking to change this.

Ormrod, Jeanne Ellis. 2003. *Educational Psychology: Developing Learners*, 4th ed. Upper Saddle River, NJ: Merrill/Prentice Hall. Educational applications of teaching and learning principles and theories.

Pak, Yoon. 2001. "Dear Teacher: Letters on the Eve of the Japanese American Imprisonment." *Middle Level Learning: Supplement to NCSS Publications* September: 10–15.

Parker, David L. 1998. *Stolen Dreams: Portraits of Working Children*. Minneapolis: Lerner Publications. Parker is a modern-day Lewis Hine who has taken numerous black-and-white photographs of working children. Describes children's situations and includes their own voices.

Paterson, Katherine. 1991. *Lyddie*. New York: Lodestar Books. In this historical fiction, Lyddie works in one of the Lowell mills and must decide whether or not to get involved in improving conditions.

Peavy, Linda, and Ursula Smith. 1999. *Frontier Children*. Norman, OK: University of Oklahoma Press. More than 200 photographs of children and many excerpts from diaries, letters, and memoirs.

Perkins, Charles. 1998. *Children of the Storm: Childhood Memories of World War II*. Osceda, WI: MEI Publishers. People from a variety of countries give firsthand accounts of their experiences.

Peterson, Scott. 2003. "Iraqi Teen Shares Her Diary of War." *Christian Science Monitor*, 2 May, 8–9.

Porter, Dorothy, ed. 1995. *Early Negro Writing 1760–1837*. Baltimore: Black Classic Press.

Prince, Mary. 1988. *The History of Mary Prince, a West Indian Slave, Related by Herself*. Reprinted in William Andrews, ed. *Six Women's Slave Narratives*. New York: Oxford University Press.

Pruzhansky, Alla. 1983. "From Russia to America in 1980." *Cobblestone*. 4 (1): 16–21. This January issue on American immigration includes eleven-year-old Alla's story of adjusting to a new life in St. Louis.

Ramsey, Alice H. 1961. *Veil, Duster, and Tire Iron*. Pasadena, CA: Castle Press. Alice describes driving her motorcar across the United States in 1909.

Rappaport, Doreen. 1993. *Tinker vs. Des Moines: Student Rights on Trial*. New York: Harper Collins. Includes a re-creation of the trial, information on the students who were involved, and photographs.

Reed, Georgia W. 1944. "Women and Children on the Oregon-California Trail in the Gold Rush Years." *Missouri Historical Review.* 39 (October): 1–23.

Reit, Seymour. 1968. *Growing Up in the White House.* New York: Crowell-Collier Press. Stories about children who lived in the White House.

Richards, Caroline Cowles. 2000. *A Nineteenth-Century Schoolgirl: The Diary of Caroline Cowles Richards, 1852–1855.* Mankato, MN: Blue Earth Books. Caroline writes about clothes, school and other activities, slavery, and hearing Susan B. Anthony speak about women's rights. This juvenile publication contains selections from Caroline's diary listed below.

———. 1997. *Village Life in America 1852–1872, Including the American Civil War as Told in the Diary of a Schoolgirl.* New York: Corner House Historical Publications.

Richardson, Judy. 1992. "Teaching *Eyes on the Prize:* Teaching Democracy." *Social Education* 56 (5): 341–345. How and why to use this video in the classroom.

Riding, Alan. 1994. "From Sarajevo, a Girl and a Diary on Fear." *New York Times* 5 January, A1, C16. A review of Zlata Filipović's diary and excerpts from an interview with her.

Roberts, W., and J. Strayer. 1996. "Empathy, Emotional Expressiveness, and Prosocial Behavior." *Child Development* 67, 449–470.

Robinson, Harriet H. 1976. *Loom and Spindle, or Life Among the Early Mill Girls.* Kailua, HA: Press Pacifica. Harriet Hanson Robinson's life beginning with her childhood working in the mills. Includes information on the *Lowell Offering* and some of its contributors.

Rochelle, Belinda. 1993. *Witnesses to Freedom: Young People Who Fought for Civil Rights.* New York: Lodestar Books. Profiles of children who were involved in the civil rights movement, including photographs and statements.

Roop, Peter, and Connie Roop. 1985. *Keep the Lights Burning, Abbie.* Minneapolis, MN: Carolrhoda Books. The true story of a young girl who took care of the lighthouse lamps by herself during a storm.

Rosenbury, Maxine. 1994. *Hiding to Survive: Stories of Jewish Children.* New York: Clarion Books. Stories of children who hid with non-Jewish families.

Ross, Pat. 1988. *Hannah's Fancy Notions: A Story of Industrial New England.* New York: Puffin Books. Historical fiction about a young girl whose sister works in a mill and who begins making hat boxes to sell.

Ruby Bridges: A Real American hero. Walt Disney Home Video. Videocassette. Although it's not a primary source, this video presents the true story of Ruby Bridges.

Russell, Marion. 1981. *Land of Enchantment: Memoirs of Marion Russell Along the Santa Fe Trail.* Albuquerque: University of New Mexico Press.

Sabuda, Robert. 1994. *Tutankhamen's Gift.* New York: Atheneum. A picture book with artwork in the style of Tutankhamen's period. Portrays Tutankhamen as a child.

Sandburg, Carl. 1953. *Prairie-Town Boy*. New York: Harcourt Brace Jovanovich. Sandburg's childhood in the midwest.

Schermerhorn, Gene. 1982. *Letters to Phil: Memories of a New York Boyhood, 1848–1856*. New York: New York Bound. In letters to his nephew, the author writes about growing up on Manhattan's West 23rd Street, when there were still farms there.

Schlissel, Lillian. 1992. *Women's Diaries of the Westward Journey*. New York: Schocken Books. Includes the diary of Rebecca Woodson, who began writing it at age fifteen, and a photocopy of a section of the diary of thirteen-year-old Barsina Rogers French showing her handwriting.

Schroeder, Alan. 1996. *Minty: A Story of Young Harriet Tubman*. New York: Dial Books for Young Readers. This picture book is a fictional story of the childhood of Harriet Tubman.

Selden, Bernice. 1983. *The Mill Girls: Lucy Larcom, Harriet Hanson Robinson, and Sarah Bagley*. New York: Atheneum. A biography of three girls who worked at the Lowell mills.

Shaftel, Fannie R., and George Shaftel. 1982. *Role Playing in the Curriculum*, 2nd ed. Englewood Cliffs, NJ: Prentice-Hall. How and why to use role playing in the classroom.

Short, Kathy, Jean Schroeder, Julie Laird, Gloria Kauffman, Margaret J. Ferguson, and Kathleen Marie Crawford. 1996. *Learning Together Through Inquiry: From Columbus to Integrated Curriculum*. York, ME: Stenhouse. Helpful ideas on using inquiry with students.

Sloane, Eric. 1986. *Eric Sloane's Sketches of America Past*. New York: Promontory Press. Contains the diary of a fifteen-year-old boy written in 1805. Sloane illustrates with drawings of tools, buildings, and other things on the farm and explains the diary's contents.

Smith, Samantha. 1985. *Samantha Smith: Journey to the Soviet Union*. Boston: Little, Brown.

Snyder, Grace. 1963. *No Time on My Hands*. Caldwell, ID: The Caxton Printers. Grace Snyder's memoir of growing up on the prairie.

Springer, Jane. 1997. *Listen to Us: The World's Working Children*. Toronto: Groundwood Books. Explains the issue of child labor and introduces young people who have been forced into labor. Includes interviews and photographs.

Stalcup, Brenda, ed. 2000. *Women's Suffrage*. San Diego: Greenhaven Press. This book, from the series Turning Points in World History, gives a brief history of the movement.

Stanley, Diane. 1995. *The True Adventures of Daniel Hall*. New York: Dial Books for Young Readers. The story of Daniel's life on a whaling ship and his efforts to return home.

Stanley, Jerry. 1992. *Children of the Dust Bowl: The True Story of the School at Weedpatch Camp*. New York: Crown. How children of families who migrated to California built their own school under the direction of Leo Hart, with photographs and quotes.

————. 1994. *I Am an American: A True Story of Japanese Internment.* New York: Crown. Includes photographs, firsthand accounts, and quotes that tell the experiences of a high school student in a relocation camp during World War II.

Stefoff, Rebecca. 1996. *Children of the Westward Trail.* Brookfield, CT: The Millbrook Press. The story of children traveling west.

Stepto, Michele. 1994. *Our Song, Our Toil: The Story of American Slavery as Told by Slaves.* Brookfield, CT: The Millbrook Press. Recollections of former slaves about their childhoods.

Stern-LaRosa, Caryl, and Ellen Hofheimer Bettmann. 2000. *Hate Hurts: How Children Learn and Unlearn Prejudice.* New York: Scholastic. The Anti-Defamation League's guide for children and adults on ways to encourage appreciation for people's differences and work against bias.

Stratton, Joanna L. 1981. *Pioneer Women: Voices from the Kansas Frontier.* New York: Simon and Schuster. A chapter titled "A Prairie Childhood" contains memoirs of people growing up on the prairie.

Strom, Yale. 1996. *Quilted Landscape: Conversations with Young Immigrants.* New York: Simon and Schuster. Children ages ten through seventeen share their experiences immigrating.

Sullivan, George. 1994. *The Day the Women Got the Vote: A Photo History of the Women's Rights Movement.* New York: Scholastic. An overall view of the struggle for suffrage.

Sunal, Cynthia S., Maria Meza, and Luisa Meza. 1994. "Children's Voices from El Salvador: War and Peace." *Social Education* 58 (1): 31–35. Describes the letter-writing activity of a fourth-grade class in San Salvador. Includes excerpts from the letters and illustrations by the children.

Takashima, Shizuye. 1989. *A Child in Prison Camp.* Plattsburg, NY: Tundra Books of Northern New York. As a child during World War II, Takashima was placed in a Canadian internment camp for people of Japanese origin.

Talayesva, Don C. 1942. *Sun Chief: The Autobiography of a Hopi Indian.* New Haven: Yale University Press. Talayesva, the Sun Chief, was reared as a Hopi Indian until he was ten and then educated by white people.

Teachers' Curriculum Institute. 1994. *History Alive! Engaging All Learners in the Diverse Classroom.* Menlo Park, CA: Addison-Wesley. Imaginative ideas for teaching history.

Tekavec, Valerie. 1997. *Teenage Refugees from Bosnia-Herzegovina Speak Out.* New York: Rosen Publishing Group. One of the books in the series In Their Own Voices: Teenage Refugees Speak Out. Young people tell their stories of what it is like to be a refugee.

————. 1995. *Teenage Refugees from Haiti Speak Out.* New York: Rosen Publishing Group. Another book in the series about teenage refugees.

Terkel, Studs. 1970. *Hard Times: An Oral History of the Great Depression.* New York: Random House.

Thomas, Martha Carey. 1979. *The Making of a Feminist*. Kent, OH: Kent State University Press.

Tillage, Leon Walter. 1997. *Leon's Story*. New York: Farrar, Straus, and Giroux. Tillage, whose father was a sharecropper in North Carolina, tells about growing up with the hatred of racism and his eventual involvement in the civil rights movement.

Tilton, George Fred. 1928. *Cap'n George Fred*. Garden City, New York: Doubleday. Tilton writes about his life as captain of a whaling ship.

Tunnell, Michael O., and George W. Chilcoat. 1996. *The Children of Topaz: The Story of a Japanese-American Internment Camp*. New York: Holiday House. Based on the diary a third-grade class kept while living at the camp in Topaz, Utah. Contains photographs of diary pages illustrated by the children and of the camp.

Tunnell, Michael O., and Richard Ammon, eds. 1985. *The Story of Ourselves: Teaching History Through Children's Literature*. Portsmouth, NH: Heinemann.

Turck, Mary C. 2000. *The Civil Rights Movement for Kids: A History with Twenty-one Activities*. Chicago: Chicago Review Press. Historical information, activities, songs, and lists of resources.

Valle-Condell, Lillian and Karen Gordon. 1986. "Teaching with Ada Millington's Diary." *Social Education*. April/May: 276–279. The authors describe how they used Ada's diary in their classrooms.

Van Der Linde, Laurel. 1993. *The Pony Express*. New York: New Discovery Books. This history of the pony express includes profiles of well-known riders, including fourteen-year-old William Cody.

Vassa, Gustavus. 2001. *The Interesting Narrative of the Life of Olaudah Equiano or Gustavus Vassa, the African, Written by Himself*. Peterborough, ONT: Broadview Press.

Vygotsky, Lev S. 1978. *Mind in Society: The Development of Higher Psychological Processes*. Cambridge, MA: Harvard University Press.

Wadsworth, Ginger. 1993. *Along the Santa Fe Trail: Marion Russell's Own Story*. Morton Grove, IL: Albert Whitman and Co. An adaptation of Russell's description in her book, *Land of Enchantment*, of her trip to Kansas in 1852 when she was seven. Beautiful illustrations.

Warren, Andrea. 1996. *Orphan Train Rider: One Boy's True Story*. Boston: Houghton Mifflin. The story of Lee Nailling, who was sent to Texas in 1926, with quotes and photographs.

———. 1998. *Pioneer Girl: Growing Up on the Prairie*. New York: Morrow Junior Books. Based on Grace McCance Snyder's memoir, *No Time on My Hands*, and includes quotes from her memoir in telling about her life as a child.

———. 2001. *We Rode the Orphan Trains*. Boston: Houghton Mifflin. Stories of orphan train riders, including many quotes from interviews with them.

Webb, Sheyann, and Rachel West Nelson. 1980. *Selma, Lord, Selma: Girlhood Memories of the Civil-Rights Days*. University, AL: The University of Alabama Press. Ten years after Sheyann Webb and Rachel West Nelson marched in Selma, they shared their recollections.

Weeks, Florence Blacow. 1859. *Notes to the Diary of Lorina Walker Weeks*. (Manuscript). Holt-Atheron Center for Western Studies, University of the Pacific, Stockton.

Weinberger, Kimberly. 2000. *Journey to a New Land: An Oral History*. New York: Mondo. The story of Elda Willitts, who immigrated from Northern Italy in 1916 when she was seven.

Welch, Catherine. 1992. *Danger at the Breaker*. Minneapolis: Carolrhoda Books. The fictional story of an eight-year-old boy who encounters dangers as he begins working in a coal mine.

Welton, David. 2002. *Children and Their World*. Boston: Houghton Mifflin Co.

Werner, Emmy E. 1995. *Pioneer Children on the Journey West*. Boulder, CO: Westview Press. Selections from children's diaries and adult memoirs about being a child traveling west.

————. 1998. *Reluctant Witnesses: Children's Voices from the Civil War*. Boulder, CO: Westview Press. Quotes from diaries, letters, and memoirs of people who were children during the war, with eyewitness accounts about children ages four to sixteen. An excellent resource, with many primary sources for teachers to select from to use in the classroom.

West, Jean M. 1989. *Child Labor in America, Vol. 3: Teaching with Primary Sources*. Peterborough, NH: Cobblestone Publishing, Inc. Contains photographs, historical documents, and a teaching guide.

West, Elliott. 1989. *Growing Up with the Country: Childhood on the Far Western Frontier*. Albuquerque: University of New Mexico Press. Uses selections from children's diaries and letters, and excerpts of memoirs to describe children's lives on the frontier.

————. 1985. "The Youngest Pioneers." *American Heritage*. (December): 90–96.

Wetterer, Margaret K. 1990. *Kate Shelley and the Midnight Express*. Minneapolis, MN: Carolrhoda Books. Kate braved a storm to warn officials that a bridge was out and helped rescue two men.

Whittaker, Alan, ed. 1988. *A Pattern of Slavery in India's Carpet Boys*. London: Anti-Slavery, International.

Wilkes, Sybella. 1994. *One Day We Had to Run! Refugee Children*. Brookfield, CT: Millbrook Press. Young Kenyan refugees communicate their experiences through paintings and words.

Willig, C. 1990. *Children's Concepts and the Primary Curriculum*. London: Paul Chapman.

Winnemucca, Sarah. 1994. *Life Among the Piutes: Their Wrongs and Claims*. Reno: University of Nevada Press.

Wisler, G. Clifton. 2001. *When Johnny Went Marching: Young Americans Fought the Civil War*. New York: HarperCollins. Stories and primary sources, including photographs, of and about boys who served.

Wister, Sally. 2000. *A Colonial Quaker Girl: The Diary of Sally Wister, 1777–1778*. Mankato, MN: Blue Earth Books. Sally, the daughter of a leading Quaker family, wrote her diary when she was sixteen.

World Book. 1998. *Stand Up for Your Rights*. Chicago: World Book. Explains each article of the Universal Declaration of Human Rights. Features interviews, stories, poems, opinions, and photographs by and of young people around the world, and explains how young people are working for human rights, with references to Peace Child International.

Yamasaki, Mitch. 1998. *Civil Rights Movement, 1954–1968: We Shall Overcome, Some Day*. Carlisle, MA: Discovery Enterprises. This book of primary sources in the Perspective on History series has a section on Little Rock.

Young, Cathy. 1989. *Growing Up in Moscow: Memories of a Soviet Girlhood*. New York: Ticknor and Fields. The author, who now lives in New Jersey, writes about her childhood in Moscow.

Zarrillo, James J. 2000. *Teaching Elementary Social Studies: Principles and Applications*. Upper Saddle River, NJ: Prentice-Hall, Inc.

Zhensun, Zheng, and Alice Low. 1991. *A Young Painter: The Life and Paintings of Wang Yani—China's Extraordinary Young Artist*. New York: Scholastic. Reproduces some of the paintings Wang Yani did from very early childhood through her teens with photographs of the artist.